The Poetry of Thomas Parnell

I0161851

Volume III – The Longer Works

The Poet Thomas Parnell was born in Ireland on 11th September 1679. He was the descendant of an ancient family, which had been settled for hundreds of years at Congleton in Cheshire. His father, also named Thomas, took the side of the Commonwealth, and at the Restoration went over to Ireland, where he purchased a considerable property. This, along with his estate in Cheshire, devolved to the poet and was to provide an income of rents with which the young Parnell could embrace life.

At school he is said to have distinguished himself by the retentiveness of his memory; often performing the task allotted for days in a few hours, and being able to repeat forty lines in any book of poems, after the first reading.

He entered Trinity College Dublin at the unusually early age of thirteen and took the degree of M.A. in 1700. The same year (although a dispensation was needed on account of his being under age) he was ordained deacon by the Bishop of Derry. Three years after, he was ordained a priest; and in 1705, he was made Archdeacon of Clogher, by Sir George Ashe, bishop of that see.

On receipt of the archdeanery, he married Miss Ann Minchin, described as a young lady of great beauty, and of an amiable character, by whom he had two sons, who tragically, died young, and a daughter, who was to survive both parents.

Up to the fall of the Whigs, at the end of Queen Anne's reign, Parnell appears to have been, like his father, a keen supporter. He now switched political allegiance to the Tories and was hailed as a valuable addition to their ranks.

Parnell was blessed with great social qualities and soon fell in with the brilliant set of literary figures; Pope, Swift, Gay. He became a member of the Scriblerus Club , an informal gathering of authors, based in London, in the early 18th century. Prominent figures from the Augustan Age of English letters were members; Jonathan Swift, Alexander Pope, John Gay, John Arbuthnot and Henry St. John. Founded in 1714 the club lasted until the death of the founders, finally ending in 1745. At about his time Parnell also wrote in the "Spectator."

To Pope, he was of essential service, assisting him in his notes to the "Iliad," being, what Pope was not, a good Greek scholar. He wrote a life of Homer, which was prefixed to the Translation, although stiff in style, and flamboyant in statement.

Parnell first visited London in 1706; and from that period till his death, scarcely a year elapsed without his spending some time in the great metropolis.

As soon as he had collected his rents, he would travel to London to enjoy himself though he continued to preach and his sermons were popular even if it appears they were more of the 'showman' type.

As each London furlough expired, he returned to Ireland, jaded and dispirited, and there took delight in nursing his melancholy; in pining for the amusements of what he had left behind; shunning and sneering at the society around him; and in abusing his native bogs and his fellow-countrymen in verse.

In 1712 he lost his wife, with whom he appears to have lived as happily as his morbid temperament and mortified feelings would permit. This blow deepened his melancholy, and drove him, it is said, to excessive drinking.

Later that same year and back in London, and once more under the "special patronage" of Dean Swift, and who wished, through his side, to mortify certain persons in Ireland, who did not appreciate, he says, the Archdeacon; and who, we suspect, besides, did not thoroughly appreciate the Dean. Swift, partly in pity for the "poor lad," as he calls him, whom he saw to be in such imminent danger of losing caste and character, and partly in the true patronising spirit, introduced Parnell to Lord Bolingbroke, who received him kindly, entertained him at dinner, and encouraged him in his poetical studies but did little else. The consequences of dissipation began, at this time, too, to appear in Parnell's constitution; and we find Swift saying of him, "His head is out of order, like mine, but more constant, poor boy." It was perhaps to this period that Pope referred, when he told Spence, "Parnell is a great follower of drams, and strangely open and scandalous in his debaucheries." If so, his bad habits seem to have sprung as much from disappointment and discontent as from taste.

Yet Swift continued to help his friend, and it was at his instance that, in 1713, Archbishop King presented Parnell with a prebend (a portion of the revenues of a cathedral or collegiate church formerly granted to a canon or member of the chapter as his stipend).

In 1714, his hope of London promotion died with Queen Anne; but in 1716, the same generous Archbishop bestowed on him the vicarage of Finglass, in the diocese of Dublin, worth £400 a-year.

However Thomas Parnell did not live long enough to enjoy the full benefit. He died at Chester, about to leave for Ireland, on 24 October 1718.

As a poet his legacy was not of the first order but his poems were greatly appreciated as were his skills as essayist and translator and obviously as a clergyman his talents seemed to have ensured promotion but quite how observant he was given his excess is difficult to judge.

Parnell's poetry is lyrical and often is written in heroic couplets. It was said of his poetry 'it was in keeping with his character, easy and pleasing, enunciating the common places with felicity and grace.' He was also one of the so-called "Graveyard poets": his 'A Night-Piece on Death,' widely considered the first "Graveyard School" poem, which was published posthumously in Poems on Several Occasions, collected and edited by his great friend Alexander Pope.

Index of Poems

David

My thought, on views of admiration hung,
Intently ravish'd and depriv'd of tongue,
Now darts a while on earth, a while in air,
Here mov'd with praise and mov'd with glory there;
The joys entrancing and the mute surprize
Half fix the blood, and dim the moist'ning eyes;
Pleasure and praise on one another break,
And Exclamation longs at heart to speak;
When thus my Genius, on the work design'd
Awaiting closely, guides the wand'ring mind.

If while thy thanks wou'd in thy lays be wrought,
A bright astonishment involve the thought,
If yet thy temper wou'd attempt to sing,
Another's quill shall imp thy feebler wing;
Behold the name of royal David near,
Behold his musick and his measures here,
Whose harp Devotion in a rapture strung,
And left no state of pious souls unsung.

Him to the wond'ring world but newly shewn,
Celestial poetry pronounc'd her own;
A thousand hopes, on clouds adorn'd with rays,
Bent down their little beauteous forms to gaze;
Fair-blooming Innocence with tender years,
And native Sweetness for the ravish'd ears,
Prepar'd to smile within his early song,
And brought their rivers, groves, and plains along;
Majestick Honour at the palace bred,
Enrob'd in white, embroider'd o'er with red,
Reach'd forth the scepter of her royal state,
His forehead touch'd, and bid his lays be great;
Undaunted Courage deck'd with manly charms,
With waving-azure plumes, and gilded arms,
Displaid the glories, and the toils of fight,
Demanded fame, and call'd him forth to write.
To perfect these the sacred spirit came,
By mild infusion of celestial flame,
And mov'd with dove like candour in his breast,
And breath'd his graces over all the rest.
Ah! where the daring flights of men aspire
To match his numbers with an equal fire;
In vain they strive to make proud Babel rise,
And with an earth-born labour touch the skies.
While I the glitt'ring page resolve to view,
That will the subject of my lines renew;
The Laurel wreath, my fames imagin'd shade,

Around my beating temples fears to fade;
My fainting fancy trembles on the brink,
And David's God must help or else I sink.

As rolling rivers in their channels flow,
Swift from aloft, but on the level slow;
Or rage in rocks, or glide along the plains,
So, just so copious, move the Psalmist's strains;
So sweetly vary'd with proportion'd heat,
So gently clear or so sublimely great,
While nature's seen in all her forms to shine,
And mix with beauties drawn from truth divine;
Sweet beauties (sweet affections endless rill,)
That in the soul like honey drops distil.

Hail holy spirit, hail supremely kind,
Whose inspirations thus enlarg'd the mind;
Who taught him what the gentle shepherd sings,
What rich expressions suit the port of kings;
What daring words describe the soldiers heat,
And what the prophet's extasies relate;
Nor let his worst condition be forgot,
In all this splendour of exulted thought.
On one thy diff'rent sorts of graces fall,
Still made for each, of equall force in all,
And while from heav'nly courts he feels a flame,
He sings the place from whence the blessing came;
And makes his inspirations sweetly prove
The tuneful subject of the mind they move.

Immortal spirit, light of life instil'd,
Who thus the bosom of a mortal fill'd,
Tho' weak my voice and tho' my light be dim,
Yet fain I'd praise thy wond'rous gifts in him;
Then since thine aid's attracted by desire,
And they that speak thee right must feel thy fire;
Vouchsafe a portion of thy grace divine,
And raise my voice and in my numbers shine;
I sing of David, David sings of thee,
Assist the Psalmist, and his work in me.

But now my verse, arising on the wing,
What part of all thy subject wilt thou sing?
How fire thy first attempt, in what resort
Of Palestina's plains, or Salem's court?
Where, as his hands the solemn measure play'd,
Curs'd fiends with torment and confusion fled;
Where, at the rosy spring of chearful light
(If pious fame record tradition right)
A soft Efflation of celestial fire
Came like a rushing breeze and shook the Lyre;

Still sweetly giving ev'ry trembling string
So much of sound as made him wake to sing.

Within my view the country first appears,
The country first enjoy'd his youthful years;
Then frame thy shady Landscapes in my strain,
Some conscious mountain or accustom'd plain;
Where by the waters, on the grass reclin'd,
With notes he rais'd, with notes he calm'd his mind;
For through the paths of rural life I'll stray,
And in his pleasures paint a shepherds day.

With grateful sentiments, with active will,
With voice exerted, and enliv'ning skill,
His free return of thanks he duely paid,
And each new day new beams of bounty shed.
Awake my tuneful harp, awake he crys,
Awake my lute, the sun begins to rise;
My God, I'm ready now! then takes a flight,
To purest Piety's exalted height;
From thence his soul, with heav'n itself in view,
On humble prayers and humble praises flew.
The praise as pleasing and as sweet the prayer,
As incense curling up thro' morning air.

When t'wards the field with early steps he trod,
And gaz'd around and own'd the works of God,
Perhaps in sweet melodious words of praise
He drew the prospect which adorn'd his ways;
The soil but newly visited with rain,
The river of the Lord with springing grain
Inlarge, encrease the soft'ned furrow blest,
The year with goodness crown'd, with beauty drest,
And still to pow'r divine ascribe it all,
From whose high paths the drops of fatness fall;
Then in the song the smiling sights rejoyce,
And all the mute creation finds a voice;
With thick returns delightful Ecchos fill
The pastur'd green, or soft ascending hill,
Rais'd by the bleatings of unnumb'red sheep,
To boast their glories in the crowds they keep;
And corn that's waving in the western gale,
With joyful sound proclaims the cover'd vale.

When e'er his flocks the lovely shepherd drove
To neighb'ring waters, to the neighb'ring grove;
To Jordan's flood refresh'd by cooling wind,
Or Cedron's brook to mossy banks confin'd,
In easy notes and guise of lowly swain,
'Twas thus he charm'd and taught the listning train.

The Lord's my Shepherd bountiful and good,
I cannot want since he provides me food;
Me for his sheep along the verdant meads,
Me all too mean his tender mercy leads;
To taste the springs of life and taste repose
Wherever living pasture sweetly grows.
And as I cannot want I need not fear,
For still the presence of my shepherd's near;
Through darksome vales where beasts of prey resort,
Where death appears with all his dreadful court,
His rod and hook direct me when I stray,
He calls to Fold, and they direct my way.

Perhaps when seated on the river's brink,
He saw the tender sheep at noon-day drink,
He sung the land where milk and honey glide
And fat'ning plenty rolls upon the tide.

Or fix'd within the freshness of a shade,
Whose boughs diffuse their leaves around his head,
He borrow'd notions from the kind retreat,
Then sung the righteous in their happy state,
And how by providential care, success
Shall all their actions in due season bless.
So firm they stand, so beautiful they look,
As planted trees aside the purling brook:
Not faded by the rays that parch the plain,
Nor careful for the want of dropping rain:
The leaves sprout forth, the rising branches shoot,
And summer crowns them with the ripen'd fruit.

But if the flow'ry field with vari'd hue
And native sweetness entertain'd his view;
The flow'ry field with all the glorious throng
Of lively colours, rose to paint his song;
Its pride and fall within the numbers ran
And spake the life of transitory man.

As grass arises by degrees unseen
To deck the breast of earth with lovely green,
'Till Nature's order brings the with'ring days,
And all the summer's beauteous pomp decays;
So by degrees unseen doth man arise,
So blooms by course and so by course he dies.
Or as her head the gawdy flowret heaves,
Spreads to the sun and boasts her silken leaves;
'Till accidental winds their glory shed,
And then they fall before the time to fade;
So man appears, so falls in all his prime,
'Ere age approaches on the steps of time.
But thee, my God! thee still the same we find,

Thy glory lasting, and thy mercy kind;
That still the just and all his race may know
No cause to mourn their swift account below.

When from beneath he saw the wand'ring sheep
That graz'd the level range along the steep,
Then rose, the wanton straglers home to call,
Before the pearly dews at ev'ning fall;
Perhaps new thoughts the rising ground supply,
And that employs his mind, which fills his eye.
From pointed hills, he crys, my wishes tend,
To that great hill from whence supports descend:
The Lord's that hill, that place of sure defence,
My wants obtain their certain help from thence.
And as large hills projected shadows throw,
To ward the sun from off the vales below,
Or for their safety stop the blasts above,
That with raw vapours loaded, nightly rove;
So shall protection o'er his servants spread,
And I repose beneath the sacred shade,
Unhurt by rage, that like a summer's day,
Destroys and scorches with impetuous ray;
By wasting sorrows undepriv'd of rest
That fall like damps by moon-shine, on the breast.
Here from the mind the prospects seem to wear,
And leave the couch'd design appearing bare;
And now no more the Shepherd sings his Hill,
But sings the sovereign Lord's protection still.
For as he sees the night prepar'd to come
On wings of ev'ning, he prepares for home,
And in the song thus adds a blessing more,
To what the thought within the figure bore:
Eternal goodness manifestly still
Preserves my soul from each approach of ill:
Ends all my days, as all my days begin,
And keeps my goings and my comings in.

Here think the sinking sun descends apace,
And from thy first attempt, my fancy, cease;
Here bid the ruddy shepherd quit the plain,
And to the fold return his flocks again.
Go, least the lyon or the shagged bear,
Thy tender lambs with savage hunger tear;
Tho' neither bear nor lyon match thy might,
When in their rage they stood reveal'd to sight;
Go, least thy wanton sheep returning home,
Shou'd as they pass thro' doubtful darkness roam.
Go ruddy youth, to Beth'lem turn thy way,
On Beth'lem's road conclude the parting day.

Methinks he goes as twilight leads the night,

And sees the Crescent rise with silver light;
His words consider all the sparkling show,
With which the stars in golden order glow.
And what is man, he crys, that thus thy kind,
Thy wond'rous love, has lodg'd him in thy mind?
For him they glitter; him the beasts of prey,
That scare my sheep, and these my sheep, obey.
O Lord, our Lord, with how deserv'd a fame,
Do's earth record the glories of thy name.
Then as he thus devoutly walks along,
And finds the road as finish'd with the song;
He sings with lifted hands and lifted eyes,
Be this, my God, an ev'ning sacrifice.

But now, the lowly dales, the trembling groves,
O'er which the whisper'd breeze serenely roves,
Leave all the course of working fancy clear,
Or only grace another subject here;
For in my purpose new designs arise,
Whose brightning images engage mine eyes.
Then here my verse thy louder accents raise,
Thy theme thro' lofty paths of glory trace,
Call forth his honours in imperial throngs
And strive to touch his more exalted songs.

While yet in humble vales his harp he strung,
While yet he follow'd after Ewes with young;
Eternal wisdom chose him for his own,
And from the flock advanc'd him to the throne;
That there his upright heart and prudent hand,
With more distinguish'd skill and high command,
Might act the shepherd in a noble sphere,
And take his nation into regal care.
He cou'd of mercy then and justice sing,
Those radiant virtues that adorn a king,
That make his reign blaze forth with bright renown,
Beyond those Gems whose splendour decks a crown:
That fixing peace, by temper'd love and fear,
Make plains abound, and barren mountains bear.
To thee to whom these attributes belong,
To thee my God, he cry'd, I send my song,
To thee from whom my regal glory came,
I sing the forms in which my court I frame;
Assist the models of imperfect skill,
O come with sacred aid, and fix my will.
A wise behaviour in my private ways,
And all my soul dispos'd to publick peace,
Shall daily strive to let my subjects see
A perfect pattern how to live in me.
Still will I think as still my glories rise,
To set no wicked thing before mine eyes.

Nor will I choose the favourites of state
Among those men that have incur'd thine hate,
Whose vice but makes 'em scandalously great;
'Tis time, that all whose froward rage of heart
Wou'd vex my realm, shall from my realm depart;
'Tis time that all whose private sland'ring lye
Leads judgment falsly, shall by judgment dye;
And time the Great who loose the reins to pride,
Shall with neglect and scorn be laid aside.
But o'er the tracts that my commands obey,
I'll send my light with sharp disarming ray,
Thro' dark retreats where humble minds abide,
Thro' shades of peace where modest tempers hide;
To find the good that may support my state,
And having found them, then to make them great.
My voice shall raise them from the lonely cell,
With me to govern and with me to dwell.
My voice shall flatt'ry and deceit disgrace,
And in their room exulted virtue place;
That with an early care and stedfast hand,
The wicked perish from the faithful land.

When on the throne he sat in calm repose,
And with a royal hope his Offspring rose,
His prayers, anticipating time, reveal
Their deep concernment for the publick weal;
Upon a good forecasted thought they run,
For common blessings in the king begun:
For righteousness and judgment strictly fair,
Which from the king descends upon his heir.
So when his life and all his labour cease,
The reign succeeding brings succeeding peace;
So still the poor shall find impartial laws,
And Orphans still a guardian of their cause:
And stern oppression have its galling yoke,
And rabid teeth of prey to pieces broke.
Then wond'ring at the glories of his way,
His friends shall love, his daunted foes obey;
For peaceful Commerce neighb'ring kings apply
And with great presents court the grand ally.
For him rich gums shall sweet Arabia bear,
For him rich Sheba, mines of gold prepare,
Him Tharsis, him the foreign isles shall greet,
And ev'ry nation bend beneath his feet.
And thus his honours far extended grow,
The type of great Messiah's reign below.

But worldly realms that in his accents shine,
Are left beneath the full advanc'd design,
When thoughts of empire in the mind encrease
O'er all the limits that determine place,

If thus the monarch's rising fancy move
To search for more unbounded realms above,
In which celestial courts the king maintains
And o'er the vast extent of nature reigns;
He then describes in elevated words,
His Israel's shepherd, as the Lord of Lords:
How bright between the Cherubims he sits,
What dazling lustre all his throne emits,
How righteousness with judgment join'd, support
The regal seat, and dignify the court.
How fairest honour and majestick state
The presence grace, and strength and beauty wait;
What glitt'ring ministers around him stand,
To fly like winds or flames at his command.
How sure the beams on which his palace rise
Are set in waters rais'd above the skies,
How wide the skies like outspread curtains fly
To vail majestick light from humane eye,
Or form'd the wide expanded vaults above,
Where storms are bounded tho' they seem to rove,
Where fire and hail and vapour so fulfil
The wise intentions of their makers will,
How well 'tis seen the great eternal mind
Rides on the clouds and walks upon the wind.

O wond'rous Lord! how bright thy glories shine,
The heav'ns declare, for what they boast is thine:
And yon blew tract, enrich'd with orbs of light,
In all its handy work displays thy might!

Again the monarch touch'd another strain,
Another province claim'd his verse again,
Where goodness infinite has fix'd a Sway,
Whose outstretch'd limits are the bounds of day.
Beneath this empire of extended air,
Yet still in reach of Providences care,
God plac'd the rounded earth with stedfast hand
And bid the basis ever firmly stand;
He bid the mountains from confusion's heaps
Exalt their summits, and assume their shapes.
He bid the waters like a garment spread,
To form large seas, and as he spake, they fled;
His voice, his thunder made the waves obey,
And forward hasten, 'till they form'd the sea;
Then least with lawless rage the surges roar,
He mark'd their bounds, and girt them in with shoar;
He fill'd the land with brooks that trembling steal
Through winding hills along the flow'ry vale,
To which the beasts that graze the vale, retreat
For cool refreshings in the summers heat;
While perch'd in leaves upon the tender sprays

The birds around their singing voices raise.
He makes the vapours which he taught to fly,
Forsake the chambers of the clouds on high,
And golden harvest rich with ears of grain,
And Spiry blades of grass adorn the plain,
And grapes luxuriant chear the soul with wine,
And ointment shed, to make the visage shine.
Through trunks of trees, fermenting sap proceeds,
To feed, and tinge the living boughs it feeds:
So shoots the firr, where airy storks abide,
So cedar, Lebanon's aspiring pride,
Whose birds by God's appointment in their nest,
With green surrounded, lye secure of rest.
Where small encrease the barren mountains give,
There kine adapted to the feeding live,
There flocks of goats in healthy pastures browse,
And in their rocky entrails rabbits house.
Where forrests thick with shrub entangled stand,
Untrod the roads and desolate the land;
There close in coverts hide the beasts of prey
'Till heavy darkness creeps upon the day,
Then roar with hunger's voice, and range abroad
And in their method seek their meat from God;
And when the dawning edge of eastern air
Begins to purple, to their dens repair.
Man next succeeding, from the sweet repose
Of downy beds, to work appointed goes;
When first the morning sees the rising sun,
He sees their labours both at once begun,
And night returning with its starry train,
Perceives their labours done at once again.
O manifold in works supremely wise,
How well thy gracious store the world supplies!
How all thy creatures on thy goodness call,
And that bestows a due support for all!
When from an open hand thy favours flow,
Rich bounty stoops to visit us below;
When from thy hand no more thy favours stream,
Back to the dust we turn from whence we came;
And when thy spirit gives the vital heat,
A sure succession keeps the kinds compleat;
The propagated seeds their forms retain,
And all the face of earth's renew'd again.
Thus, as you've seen th' effect reveal the cause,
Is nature's ruler known in nature's laws;
Thus still his pow'r is o'er the world display'd
And still rejoices in the world he made.
The Lord he reigns, the king of kings is king,
Let nations praise, and praises learn to sing.

My verses here may change their stile again,

And trace the Psalmist in another strain;
Where all his soul the soldiers spirit warms,
And to the musick fits the sound of arms,
Where brave disorder does in numbers dwell,
And artful number speaks disorder well.
Arise my genius and attempt the praise
Of dreaded pow'r and perilous essays,
And where his accents are too nobly great,
Like distant ecchos give the faint repeat.
For who like him with enterprizing pen,
Can paint the Lord of Hosts in wrath with men,
Or with just images of tuneful lay
Set all his terrors in their fierce array?
He comes! The tumult of discording spheres,
The quiv'ring shocks of earth, confess their fears;
Thick smoaks precede, and blasts of angry breath
That kindle dread devouring flames of death.
He comes! the firmament with dismal night
Bows down, and seems to fall upon the light,
The darkling mists inwrap his head around,
The waters deluge and the tempests sound,
While on the cherub's purple wings he flys,
And plants his black pavilion in the skies.
He comes! the clouds remove, the rattling hail
Descending, bounds and scatters o'er the vale;
His voice is heard, his thunder speaks his ire,
His light'ning blasts with blue sulphurious fire,
His brandish'd bolts with swift commission go
To punish man's rebellious acts below.
His stern rebukes lay deepest ocean bare,
And solid earth by wide eruption tear;
Then glares the naked gulph with dismal ray,
And then the dark foundations see the day.
O God! let mercy this thy war asswage,
Alas! no mortal can sustain thy rage.

While I but strive the dire effects to tell,
And on another's words attentive dwell,
Confusing passions in my bosom roll,
And all in tumult work the troubled soul:
Remorse with pity, fear with sorrow blend,
And I but strive in vain; my verse, descend,
To less aspiring paths direct thy flight,
Tho' still the less may more than match thy might,
While I to second agents tune the strings,
And Israel's warrior, Israel's battles sings;
Great warrior he, and great to sing of war,
Whose lines (if ever lines prevail'd so far)
Might pitch the tents, compose the ranks anew,
To combat sound, and bring the toil to view.
O nation most securely rais'd in name,

Whose fair records he wrote for endless fame;
O nation oft victorious o'er thy foes,
At once thy conquests and thy thanks he shews;
For thus he sung the realms that must be thine
And made thee thus confess an aid divine.
When mercy look'd, the waves perceiv'd its sway,
And Israel pass'd the deep divided sea.
When mercy spake it, haughty Pharoah's host
And haughty Pharoah by the waves were tost.
When mercy led us through the desart sand,
We reach'd the borders of the promis'd land:
Then all the kings their gather'd armies brought,
And all those kings by mercy's help we fought:
There with their monarch Amor's people bleed,
For God was gracious, and the tribes succeed.
There monst'rous Ogg was fell'd on Basan's plain,
For God was gracious to the tribes again.
At length their yoke the realms of Canaan feel,
And Israel sings that God is gracious still.

Nor has the warlike prince alone enroll'd
The wond'rous feats their fathers did of old;
His own emblazon'd acts adorn his lays,
These too may challenge just returns of praise.
My God! he crys, my surest rock of might,
My trust in dangers and my shield in fight,
Thy matchless bounties I with gladness own,
Nor find assistance but from thee alone;
Thy strength is armour, and my path success,
No pow'r like thee can thus securely bless;
When troops united wou'd arrest my course,
I break their files, and through their order force;
When in their towns they keep, my seige I form,
And leap the battlements, and lead the storm;
And when in camps abroad intrench'd they lye,
As swift as hinds in chace I bound on high;
My strenuous arms thou teachest how to kill,
And snap in sunder temper'd bows of steel;
My moving footsteps are enlarg'd by thee,
And kept from snares of planned ambush free;
And when my foes forsake the field of fight,
Then flush'd with conquest I pursue their flight;
In vain their fears that almost reach despair,
The trembling wretches from mine anger bear;
As swift as fear brisk warmth of conquest goes,
And at my feet dejects the wounded foes;
For help they call, but find their helper's gone,
For God's against them, and I drive them on:
As whirling dust in airy tumult fly
Before the tempest that involves the sky;
And in my rage's unavoided sway,

I tread their necks like abject heaps of clay.

The warriour thus in song his deeds express'd,
Nor vainly boasted what he but confess'd,
While warlike actions were proclaim'd abroad,
That all their praises, shou'd refer to God.

And here to make this bright design arise
In fairer splendor to the nation's eyes,
From private valour he converts his lays,
For yet the publick claim'd attempts of praise,
And publick conquests where they jointly fought,
Thus stand recorded by reflecting thought;
God sent his Samuel from his holy seat
To bear the promise of my future state,
And I rejoicing see the tribes fulfil
The promis'd purpose of almighty will;
Subjected Sichem, sweet Samaria's plain,
And Succoth's valleys have confess'd my reign;
Remoter Gilead's hilly tracts obey,
Manasseh's parted sands accept my sway;
Strong Ephraim's sons, and Ephraim's ports are mine,
And mine the throne of princely Judah's line;
Then since my people with my standard go,
To bring the strength of adverse empire low:
Let Moab's soil, to vile subjection brought,
With groans declare how well our ranks have fought;
Let vanquish'd Edom bow its humbled head,
And tell how pompous on its pride I tread;
And now Philistia with thy conqu'ring host,
Dismaid and broke, of conquer'd Israel boast;
But if a Seir or Rabbah yet remain
On Johemaan's Hill, or Ammon's plain,
Lead forth our armies Lord, regard our prayer,
Lead Lord of battles and we'll conquer there.
As this the warrior spake, his heart arose,
And thus with grateful turn perform'd the close;
Though men to men their best assistance lend,
Yet men alone will but in vain befriend,
Through God we work exploits of high renown,
'Tis God that treads our great opposers down.

Hear now the praise of well disputed fields,
The best return victorious honour yields;
'Tis common good restor'd, when lovely peace
Is join'd with righteousness in strict embrace;
Hear all ye victors what your sword secures,
Hear all you nations for the cause is yours;
And when the joyful trumpets loudly sound,
When groaning captives in their ranks are bound;
When pillars lift the bloody plumes in air,

And broken shafts and batter'd armour bear,
When painted arches acts of war relate,
When slow procession's pomps augment the state,
When fame relates their worth among the throng,
Thus take from David their triumphant song;
Oh clap your hands together, Oh rejoice
In God with melody's exalted voice,
Your sacred Psalm within his dwelling raise,
And for a pure oblation offer praise,
For the rich goodness plentifully shews,
He prospers our design upon our foes.
Then hither all ye nations hither run,
Behold the wonders which the Lord has done,
Behold with what a mind, the heap of slain,
He spreads the sanguine surface of the plain,
He makes the wars that mad confusion hurl'd,
Be spent in victories, and leave the world.
He breaks the bended bows, the spears of Ire,
And burns the shatter'd chariots in the Fire,
And bids the realms be still, the tumult cease,
And know the Lord of war, for Lord of peace;
Now may the tender youth in goodness rise,
Beneath the guidance of their parents eyes,
As tall young poplars when the rangers nigh,
To watch their risings least they shoot awry.
Now may the beauteous Daughters bred with care,
In modest rules and pious acts of fear,
Like polish'd corners of the Temple be,
So bright, so spotless, and so fit for thee.
Now may the various seasons bless the soil,
And plenteous Garners pay the Ploughman's toil;
Now sheep and kine upon the flow'ry meads,
Encrease in thousands and ten thousand heads,
And now no more the sound of grief complains,
For those that fall in fight, or live in chains;
Here when the blessings are proclaim'd aloud,
Join all the voices of the thankful crowd,
Let all that feel them thus confess their part,
Thus own their worth with one united heart;
Happy the realm which God vouchsafes to bless
With all the glories of a bright success!
And happy thrice the realm if thus he please,
To crown those glories with the sweets of ease.

From warfare finish'd, on a chain of thought
To bright attempts of future rapture wrought;
Yet stronger, yet thy pinnions stronger raise,
Oh fancy, reigning in the pow'r of lays.
For Sion's Hill thine airy courses hold,
'Twas there thy David Prophecy'd of old,
And there devout in contemplation sit,

In holy vision and extatick fit.

Methinks I seem to feel the charm begin,
Now sweet contentment tunes my soul within,
Now wond'rous soft arising musick plays,
And now full sounds upon the sense encrease;
Tis David's Lyre, his artful fingers move,
To court the spirit from the realms above,
And pleas'd to come where holiness attends,
The courted spirit from above descends.
Hence on the Lyre and voice new graces rest,
And bright Prophetick forms enlarge the breast;
Hence firm decrees his mystick Hymns relate,
Affix'd in Heav'ns adamantine gate,
The glories of the most important age,
And Christ's blest empire seen by sure presage.

When in a distant view with inward eyes,
He sees the Son descending from the skies,
To take the form of Man for Mankind's sake,
Tis thus he makes the great Messiah speak:
It is not, Father, blood of bullocks slain
Can cleanse the World from universal stain,
Such Off'rings are not here requir'd by thee,
But point at mine, and leave the work for me;
To perfect which, as Servants ears they drill,
In sign of op'ning to their Masters will,
Thy will wou'd open mine, and have me bear,
My sign of Ministry, the body there.
Prophetick volumes of our state assign
The worlds redemption as an act of mine,
And lo, with chearful and obedient heart,
I come, my father, to perform my part.
So spake the Son, and left his throne above,
When wings to bear him were prepar'd by love,
When with their Monarch on the great descent,
Sweet humbleness and gentle patience went,
Fair sisters both, both bless'd in his esteem,
And both appointed here to wait on him.

But now before the Prophet's ravish'd eyes,
Succeeding Prospects of his Life arise,
And here he teaches all the world to sing,
Those strains in which the nation own'd him King.
When boughs as at an holy feast they bear,
To shew the Godhead manifested there;
And garments as a mark of glory strow'd,
Declar'd a Prince proclaim'd upon the road;
This day the Lord hath made we will employ
In songs, he crys, and consecrate to joy.
Hosannah, Lord, Hosannah, shed thy peace,

Hosannah, long expecting nations grace,
Oh, bless'd in honour's height triumphant, thou
That wast to come, Oh bless thy people now.

Twere easy dwelling here with fix'd delight,
And much the sweet engagement of the sight;
But fleeting visions each on other throng,
And change the musick and demand the song.
Ah! musick chang'd by sadly moving show,
Ah! song demanded in excess of woe!
For what was all the gracious Saviour's stay,
Whilst here he trod in Life's encumber'd way,
But troubled patience, persecuted breath,
Neglected sorrows, and afflicting death?
Approach ye sinners, think the garden shews
His bloody sweat of full arising throes,
Approach his grief, and hear him thus complain
Through David's person, and in David's strain.

Oh save me God, thy floods about me roll,
Thy wrath divine hath overflow'd my soul,
I come at length where rising waters drown,
And sink in deep affliction deeply down.
Deceitful snares to bring me to the dead,
Lye ready plac'd in ev'ry path I tread;
And Hell itself, with all that Hell contains,
Of fiends accurs'd, and dreadful change of pains;
To daunt firm will, and cross the good design'd,
With strong temptations fasten on the mind;
Such grief such sorrows in amazing view,
Distracted fears and heaviness pursue.
Ye sages deeply read in human frame,
The passions causes, and their wild extream,
Where mov'd an object more oppos'd to bliss,
What other agony cou'd equal his?

The musick still proceeds with mournful airs,
And speaks the dangers, as it speaks the fears.
Oh sacred Presence from the son withdrawn,
Oh God my father wither art thou gone?
Oh must my soul bewail tormenting pain,
And all my words of anguish fall in vain?
The trouble's near in which my life will end,
But none is near that will assistance lend;
Like Basan's bulls my foes against me throng
So proud, inhuman, numberless, and strong.
Like desart lyons on their prey they go,
So much their fierce desire of blood they shew:
As ploughers wound the ground, they tore my back
And long deep furrows manifest the track.
They pierc'd my tender hands, my tender feet,

And caus'd sharp pangs, where nerves in numbers meet;
Rich streams of life forsake my rended veins
And fall like water spill'd upon the plains;
My bones that us'd in hollow seats to close,
Disjoint with anguish of convulsive throes;
My mourning heart is melted in my frame
As wax dissolving runs before a flame,
My strength dries up, my flesh the moisture leaves,
And on my tongue my clammy palate cleaves.
Alass! I thirst, alass! for drink I call,
For drink they give me vinegar and gall.
To sportful game the savage soldiers go
And for my vesture on my vesture throw;
While all deride who see me thus forlorn
And shoot their lips and shake their heads in scorn.
And with despiteful jest, behold, they cry,
The great peculiar darling of the sky,
He trusted God wou'd save his soul from woe,
Now God may have him if he loves him so.
But to the dust of death by quick decay
I come, O Father, be not long away.
And was it thus the prince of life was slain?
And was it thus he dy'd for worthless men?
Yes blessed Jesus! thus in ev'ry line
These suff'rings which the Prophet spake were thine.

Come christian to the corps, in spirit come,
And with true signs of grief surround the tomb.
Upon the threshold stone let sin be slain,
Such sacrifice will best avenge his pain.
Bring thither then repentance, sighs and tears,
Bring mortify'd desires, bring holy fears;
And earnest pray'r express'd from thoughts that roll
Through broken mind, and groanings of the soul;
These scatter on his hearse, and so prepare
Those obsequies the Jews deny'd him there,
While in your hearts the flames of love may burn,
To dress the vault, like lamps in sacred urn.
There oft my soul in such a grateful way,
Thine humblest homage with the godly pay.

But David strikes the sounding chords anew,
And to thy first design recalls thy view;
From life to death, from death to life he flies
And still pursues his object in his eyes.
And here recounts in more enliven'd song
The sacred Presence, not absented long.
The flesh not suffer'd in the grave to dwell,
The soul not suffer'd to remain in hell;
But as the conqueror fatigu'd in war,
With hot pursuit of enemies afar,

Reclines to drink the torrent gliding by,
Then lifts his looks to repossess the sky,
So bow'd the Son in life's uneasy road,
With anxious toil, and thorny danger strew'd;
So bow'd the son, but not to find relief,
But taste the deep imbitter'd floods of grief;
So when he tasted these he rais'd his head,
And left the sabled mansions of the dead,
Ere mould'ring time consum'd the bones away,
Or slow corruption's worms had work'd decay;
Here faith's foundations, all the soul employ
With springing graces, springing beams of joy,
Then paus'd the voice where nature's seen to pause,
And for a time suspend her ancient laws.

From hence arising as the glories rise,
That must advance above the lofty skies,
He runs with sprightly fingers o'er the Lyre,
And fills new songs with new celestial fire:
In which he shews by fair description's ray,
The Christ's Ascension, to the realms of day;
When Justice, pleas'd with life already paid,
Unbends her brows, and sheaths her angry blade;
And meditates rewards, and will restore
What mercy woo'd him to forsake before,
When on a cloud with gilded edge of light,
He rose above the reach of human sight,
And met the pomp that hung aloft in air
To make his honours more exceeding fair.
See, cries the prophet, how the chariots wait
To bear him upwards in triumphant state,
By twenty thousands in unnumber'd throng,
And Angels draw the glitt'ring ranks along.
The Lord amongst them sits in glory dress'd,
Nor more the Presence Sinai mount confest.
And now the chariots have begun to fly,
The triumph moves, the Lord ascends on high,
And Sin and Satan, us'd to captive men,
Are dragg'd for captives in his ample train;
While as he goes seraphick circles sing
The wond'rous conquest of their wond'rous king,
With shouts of joy their heav'nly voices raise,
And with shrill trumpets manifest his praise.
From such a point of such exceeding height
A while my verses stoop their airy flight,
And seem for rest on Olivet to breath,
And charge the two that stand in white beneath,
That as they move and join the moving rear,
Within their honour'd hands aloft they bear
The crown of thorns, the cross on which he dy'd,
The nails that pierc'd his limbs, the spear his side;

Then where kind mercy lays the thunder by,
Where Peace has hung great Michael's arms on high,
Let these adorn his magazine above,
And hang the trophies of victorious love,
Least man by superstitious mind entic'd,
Shou'd idolize whatever touch'd the Christ.

But still the Prophet in the spirit soars
To new Jerusalem's imperial doors;
There sees and hears the bless'd angelick throng,
There feels their musick, and records their song:
Or with the vision warm'd, attempts to write
For those inhabitants of native light,
And teaches harmony's distinguish'd parts,
In sweet respondence of united hearts;
For thus without might warbling angels sing,
Their course containing on the flutter'd wing;
Eternal gates! your stately portals rear,
Eternal gates! your ways of joy prepare,
The king of glory for admittance stays,
He comes, he'll enter, O prepare your ways;
Then bright arch-angels that attend the wall,
Might thus upon the beauteous order call;
Ye fellow ministers that now proclaim
Your king of glory, tell his awful name.
At which the beauteous order will accord,
And sound of solemn notes pronounce the Lord,
The Lord endew'd with strength, renown'd for might,
With spoils returning from the finish'd fight.
Again with Lays they charm the sacred gates,
And graces double while the song repeats,
Again within the sacred guardians sing,
And ask the name of their victorious king,
And then again the Lord's the name rebounds
From tongue to tongue, catch'd up in frequent rounds.

New thrones and pow'rs appear, to lift the gate,
And David still pursues their enter'd state;
Oh prophet! father! whither woudst thou fly?
Oh mystick Israel's chariot for the sky,
Thou sacred spirit! what a wond'rous height,
By thee supported, soars his airy flight!
For glimpse of Majesty divine is brought,
Among the shifted prospects of the thought;
Dread sacred sight! I dare not gaze for fear,
But sit beneath the singers feet and hear,
And hold each sound that interrupts the mind,
Thus in a calm by pow'r of verse confin'd.

Ye dreadful ministers of God, displeas'd,
Loud blasting tempests, be no longer rais'd!

Ye deep mouth'd thunders leave your direful groan,
Nor roll in hollow clouds around the throne,
The still small voice more justly will express
How great Jehovah did the Lord address,
And you bright feather'd choirs of endless peace,
A while from tuneful Hallelujahs cease,
A while stand fix'd with deep attentive care,
You'll have the time to sing for ever there.
The royal prophet will the silence break,
And in his words almighty goodness speak.
He spake (and smil'd to see the business done,)
Thou art my first, my great begotten son;
Here on the right of Majesty sit down,
Enjoy thy conquest and receive thy crown,
While I thy worship and renown compleat,
And make thy foes the foot-stool of thy feet,
For I'll pronounce the long resolv'd decree,
My sacred Sion be reserv'd for thee.
From thence thy peaceful rod of pow'r extend,
From thence thy messenger of mercy send,
And teach thy vanquish'd enemies to bow,
And rule where Hell has fix'd an empire now.
Then ready nations to their rightful king,
The free-will off'rings of their hearts shall bring,
In holy beauties for acceptance dress'd,
And ready nations be with pardon bless'd;
Mean while thy dawn of truth begins the day,
Enlightened subjects shall encrease thy sway,
With such a splendid and unnumber'd train,
As dews in morning fill the grassy plain.
This by myself I swore; the great intent
Has past my sanction and I can't repent;
Thou art a king and priest of peace below,
Like Salem's monarch and for ever so.
Ask what thou wilt, 'tis thine; the gentiles claim,
For thy possession take the world's extream,
The kings shall rage, the parties strive in vain,
By persecuting rage to break thy reign;
Thou art my Christ and they that still can be
Rebellious subjects, be destroy'd by thee.
Bring like the Potter to severe decay,
Thy worthless creatures, found in humble clay.
Then hear ye monarchs, and ye judges hear,
Rejoice with trembling, serve the Lord with fear,
In his commands with signs of homage move,
And kiss the gracious offers of his love;
Ye surely perish if his anger flame,
And only they be bless'd that bless his name.
Thus does the Christ in David's anthems shine,
With full magnificence of art divine,
Then on his subjects gifts of grace bestow,

And spread his Image on their hearts below,
As when our earthly kings receive the globe,
The sacred unction and the purple robe,
And mount the throne with golden glory crown'd,
They scatter medals of themselves around;
There heav'nly singers clap their vary'd wings,
And lead the choir of all created things,
Relate his glory's everlasting prime,
His fame continu'd with the length of time,
While e're the Sun shall dart a gilded beam,
Or changing Moons diffuse the silver'd gleam,
Where e're the waves of rolling ocean sent,
Encompass land with arms of wide extent.
Hail, full of mercy, ready nations cry!
Hail, for ever, ever bless'd on high!
Hail, Oh for ever on thy beauteous throne!
Thou Lord that workest wond'rous things alone,
Still let thy glory to the world appear,
And all the riches of thy goodness hear.

But thou fair Church in whom he fixes love,
Thou queen accepted of the prince above;
Behold him fairer than the sons of men,
Embrace his offer'd heart, and share his reign;
In Moses's laws they bred thy tender years,
But now to new commands incline thine ears,
Forget thy people, bear no more in mind
Thy Father's houshold, for thy spouse is kind.
Within thy soul let vain affections dye,
Him only worship, and with him comply.
So shall thy spouse's heart with thine agree,
So shall his fervour still encrease for thee.
Come while he calls, supremely favour'd queen,
In heav'nly glories dress thy soul within;
With pious actions to the throne be brought,
In close connection of the virtues wrought,
Let these around thee for a garment shine,
And be the work to make them pleasing, thine:
Come, lovely queen, advance with stately port,
Thy good companions shall compleat thy court,
With joyful souls their joyful entrance sing,
And fill the palace of your gracious king.
What tho' thy Moses and the prophets cease,
What tho' the Priesthood leaves the settled race,
The Father's place their offspring well supplies,
When at thy spouse's Ministry they rise,
When thy bless'd houshold on his orders go,
And rule for him where'er he reigns below.
Come, Queen exalted, come, my lasting song
To future ages shall thy fame prolong.
The joyful nations shall thy praise proclaim,

And for their safety crowd beneath thy name.
Oh bounteous Saviour! still thy mercy kind,
Still what thy David sung, thy servants find,
Still why thy David sung thy servants see,
From thee sent down, and sent again to thee.
They see the words of thanks and love divine,
In strains mysterious intermingl'd shine,
As sweet and rich unite in costly waves,
When purling gold the purpled webb receives,
And still the Church he shadow'd hears the lays,
In daily service as an aid to praise.
At these her temper good devotion warms,
And mounts aloft with more engaging charms.
Then as she strives to reach the lofty sky,
Bids gratitude assist her will to fly;
In these our gratitude becomes on fire,
Then feels its flames improv'd by strong desire,
Then feels desire in eager wishes move,
And wish determine in the point of love.

Such hymns to regulate and such to raise,
Approach, ye sounding instruments of praise.
Tis fit you tune for him whose holy love,
In wish aspiring to the choir above,
And fond to practice e're his time to go,
Devoutly call'd you to the choir below;
There where he plac'd you, with your solemn sound,
For Gods high glory fill the sacred ground,
And there and ev'ry where his wond'rous name,
Within his firmament of pow'r proclaim.
Soft pleasing lutes with easy sweetness move,
To touch the sentiments of Heav'nly love,
Assist the Lyre and voice to tell the charms
That gently stole him from the Father's arms;
Gay trembling Timbrels us'd with airs of mirth,
Assist the loud Hosannah rais'd on earth,
When on an Ass he meekly rides along,
And multitudes are heard within the song.
Full-tenor'd Psalt'ry, join the doleful part,
In which his agony possest his heart;
And seem to feel thyself, and seem to shew,
Arising heaviness and signs of woe.
Sonorous organ at his passion moan,
And utter forth thy sympathizing groan,
In big slow murmurs anxious sorrow speak,
While melancholy winds thine entrails shake,
As when he suffer'd, with complaining sound,
The storms in vaulted caverns shook the ground;
Swift chearful cymbals give an airy strain,
When having bravely broke the doubled chain,
Of Death and Hell, he left the conquer'd grave,

And rose to visit those he dy'd to save.
And as he mounts in song and Angels sing
With grand procession their returning king,
Triumphant trumpets raise their notes on high,
And make them seem to mount, and seem to fly.
Then all at once conspire to praise the Lord,
In musick's full consent, and just accord:
Ye sons of art, in such melodious way
Conclude the service which you join to pay,
While nations sing Amen, and yet again,
Hold forth the note and sing aloud Amen.

Here has my fancy gone where David leads,
Now softly pacing o'er the grassy meads,
Now nobly mounting where the monarchs rear
The gilded spires of palaces in air,
Now shooting thence upon the level flight,
To dreadful dangers and the toils of fight,
Anon with utmost stretch ascending far,
Beyond the region of the farthest star;
As sharpest sighted eagles tow'ring fly,
To weather their broad sails in open sky,
At length on wings half clos'd slide gently down,
And one attempt shall all my labours crown.
In other's verse the rest be better shewn,
But this is more, or should be more, thine own.

If then the spirit that supports my lines,
Have prov'd unequal to my large designs,
Let others rise from earthly passion's dream,
By me provok'd to vindicate the theme.
Let others round the world in rapture rove,
Or with strong feathers fan the breeze above,
Or walk the dusky shades of death, and dive
Down Hell's abyss, and mount again alive.
But Oh my God! may these unartful rhimes,
In sober words of woe bemoan my crimes.
Tis fit the sorrows I for ever vent,
For what I never can enough repent;
Tis fit, and David shews the moving way,
And with his pray'r instructs my soul to pray.
Then since thy guilt is more than match'd by me,
And since my troubles shou'd with thine agree,
O Muse to glories in affliction born!
May thine humility my soul adorn.
For humblest prayers are most affecting strains,
As Mines lye rich in lowly planted veins;
Such aid I want to render mercy kind,
And such an aid as here I want I find:
Thy weeping accents in my numbers run,
Ah thought! ah voice of inward dole begun!

My God, whose anger is appeas'd by tears,
Bow gently down thy mercy's gracious ears;
With many tongues my sins for justice call,
But mercy's ears are manifold for all.
Those sweet celestial windows open wide,
And in full streams let soft compassion glide,
There wash my soul and cleanse it yet again,
O th'roughly cleanse it from the guilty stain,
For I my life with inward anguish see,
And all its wretchedness confess to thee.
The large Inditement stands before my view,
Drawn forth by conscience, most amazing true,
And fill'd with secrets hid from human eye,
When foolish man, thy God stood witness by.
Then Oh, thou majesty divinely great,
Accept the sad confessions I repeat,
Which clear thy justice to the world below,
Shou'd dismal sentence doom my soul to woe.
When in the silent womb my shape was made,
And from the womb to lightsome life convey'd,
Curs'd sin began to take unhappy root,
And thro' my veins its early fibres shoot;
And then what goodness did'st thou shew, to kill
The rising weeds, and principles of ill;
When to my breast in fair celestial flame,
Eternal truth and lovely wisdom came,
Bright gift by simple nature never got,
But here reveal'd to change the antient blot.
This wond'rous help which mercy pleas'd to grant,
Continue still, for still thine aid I want,
And as the men whom leprosies invade,
Or they that touch the carcase of the dead,
With Hysop sprinkled and by water clean'd,
Their former pureness in the law regain'd;
So purge my soul diseas'd alas! within,
And much polluted with dead works of sin.
For such bless'd favours at thine hand I sue,
Be grace thine Hysop and thy water too.
Then shall my whiteness for perfection vie
With blanching snows that newly leave the sky.
Thus through my mind thy voice of gladness send,
Thus speak the joyful word, I will be clean'd;
That all my strength consum'd with mournful pain,
May by thy saving health rejoice again:
And now no more my foul offences see,
Oh turn from these, but turn thee not from me,
Or least they make me too deform'd a sight,
Oh, blot them with oblivion's endless night.
Then further pureness to thy servant grant,
Another heart, or change in this, I want.

Create another, or the change create,
For now my vile corruption is so great,
It seems a new creation to restore
Its fall'n estate to what it was before.
Renew my spirit, raging in my breast,
And all its passions in their course arrest,
Or turn their motions, widely gone astray,
And fix their footsteps in thy righteous way.
When this is granted, when again I'm whole,
Oh ne'er withdraw thy presence from my soul:
There let it shine, so let me be restor'd
To present joy which conscious hopes afford.
There let it sweetly shine, and o'er my breast
Diffuse the dawning of eternal rest;
Then shall the wicked this compassion see,
And learn thy worship and thy works from me.
For I to such occasions of thy praise
Will tune my lyre, and consecrate my lays.
Unseal my lips, where guilt and shame have hung
To stop the passage of my grateful tongue,
And let my prayer and song ascend, my prayer
Here join'd with saints, my song with angels there;
Yet neither prayer I'd give, nor songs alone,
If other off'rings were as much thy own:
But thine's the contrite spirit, thine's an heart
Oppress'd with sorrow, broke with inward smart;
That at thy footstool in confession shews
How well its faults, how well the judge it knows;
That sin with sober resolution flies,
This gift thy mercy never will despise.
Then in my soul a mystick altar rear,
And such a sacrifice I'll offer there;
There shall it stand in vows of virtue bound,
There falling tears shall wash it all around;
And sharp remorse, yet sharper edg'd by woe,
Deserv'd and fear'd, inflict the bleeding blow;
There shall my thoughts to holy breathings fly
Instead of incense to perfume the sky,
And thence my willing heart aspires above,
A victim panting in the flames of love.

Jonah

Thus sung the king—some angel reach a bough
From Eden's tree to crown the wisest brow;
And now thou fairest garden ever made,
Broad banks of spices, blossom'd walks of shade,
O Lebanon! where much I love to dwell,
Since I must leave thee Lebanon, farewel!

Swift from my soul the fair Idea flies,
A wilder sight the changing scene supplies,
Wide seas come rolling to my future page,
And storms stand ready when I call, to rage.
Then go where Joppa crowns the winding shore,
The prophet Jonah just arrives before,
He sees a ship unmooring, soft the gales,
He pays, and enters, and the vessel sails.

Ah wou'dst thou fly thy God? rash man forbear,
What land so distant but thy God is there?
Weak reason, cease thy voice.—They run the deep,
And the tir'd prophet lays his limbs to sleep.
Here God speaks louder, sends a storm to sea,
The clouds remove to give the vengeance way;
Strong blasts come whistling, by degrees they roar
And shove big surges tumbling on to shore;
The vessel bounds, then rolls, and ev'ry blast
Works hard to tear her by the groaning mast;
The sailors doubling all their shouts and cares
Furl the white canvas, and cast forth the wares,
Each seek the God their native regions own,
In vain they seek them, for those Gods were none.
Yet Jonah slept the while, who solely knew,
In all that number, where to find the true.
To whom the pilot: sleeper, rise and pray,
Our Gods are deaf; may thine do more than they.

But thus the rest: perhaps we waft a foe
To heav'n itself, and that's our cause of woe;
Let's seek by lots, if heav'n be pleas'd to tell;
And what they sought by lots, on Jonah fell:
Then whence he came, and who, and what, and why
Thus rag'd the tempest, all confus'dly cry,
Each press'd in haste to get his question heard,
When Jonah stops them with a grave regard.

An Hebrew man you see, who God revere,
He made this world, and makes this world his care,
His the whirl'd sky, these waves that lift their head,
And his yon land, on which you long to tread.
He charg'd me late, to Nineveh repair,
And to their face denounce his sentence there:
Go, said the vision, prophet, preach to all,
Yet forty days and Nineveh shall fall.
But well I knew him gracious to forgive,
And much my zeal abhor'd the bad shou'd live,
And if they turn they live; then what were I
But some false prophet when they fail to die?
Or what I fanci'd had the Gentiles too

With Hebrew prophets, and their God to do?
Drawn by the wilful thoughts, my soil I run,
I fled his presence and the work's undone.

The storm increases as the prophet speaks,
O'er the toss'd ship a foaming billow breaks,
She rises pendant on the lifted waves
And thence descries a thousand watry graves,
Then downward rushing, watry mountains hide
Her hulk beneath in deaths on ev'ry side.
O, cry the sailors all, thy fact was ill,
Yet, if a prophet, speak thy master's will,
What part is ours with thee? can ought remain
To bring the blessings of a calm again?

Then Jonah—mine's the death will best atone
(And God is pleas'd that I pronounce my own)
Arise and cast me forth, the wind will cease,
The sea subsiding wear the looks of peace,
And you securely steer. For well I see
Myself the criminal, the storm for me.

Yet pity moves for one that owns a blame,
And awe resulting from a prophet's name;
Love pleads, he kindly meant for them to die,
Fear pleads against him, lest they pow'r defy:
If then to aid the flight abets the sin,
They think to land him, where they took him in.
Perhaps to quit the cause might end the woe,
And God appeasing, let the vessel go.
For this they fix their oars and strike the main,
But God withstands them, and they strike in vain.

The storm increases more with want of light,
Low black'ning clouds involve the ship in night,
Thick batt'ring rains fly thro' the driving skies,
Loud thunder bellows, darted light'ning flies,
A dreadful picture night-born horrour drew,
And his, or theirs, or both their fates, they view.

Then thus to God they cry; Almighty pow'r,
Whom we ne'er knew 'till this despairing hour,
From this devoted blood thy servants free,
To us he's innocent, if so to thee;
In all the past we see thy wond'rous hand,
And that he perish, think it thy command.

This pray'r perform'd, they cast the prophet o'er,
A surge receives him and he mounts no more;
Then stills the thunder, cease the flames of blue,
The rains abated and the winds withdrew,

The clouds ride off, and as they march away,
Thro' ev'ry breaking shoots a chearful day;
The sea, which rag'd so loud, accepts the prize,
A while it rolls, then all the tempest dies,
By gradual sinking, flat the surface grows,
And safe the vessel with the sailors goes.
The Lion thus, that bounds the fences o'er,
And makes the Mountain-Ecchoes learn to roar,
If on the lawn a branching deer he rend,
Then falls his hunger, all his roarings end,
Murm'ring a while, to rest his limbs he lays,
And the freed lawn enjoys its herd at ease.

Bless'd with the sudden calm, the sailors own
That wretched Jonah worship'd right alone,
Then make their vows, the victim sheep prepare,
Bemoan the prophet, and the God revere.

Now tho' you fear to loose the pow'r to breath,
Now tho' you tremble, Fancy, dive beneath;
What world of wonders in the deep are seen;
But this the greatest—Jonah lives within!
The man who fondly fled the Maker's view,
Strange as the crime has found a dungeon too.
God sent a monster of the frothing sea,
Fit by the bulk to gorge the living prey,
And lodge him still alive; this hulk receives
The falling prophet as he dash'd the waves.
There newly wak'd, from fanci'd death he lies,
And oft again in apprehension dies:
While three long days and nights depriv'd of sleep,
He turn'd and toss'd him up and down the deep.
He thinks the judgment of the strangest kind,
And much he wonders what the Lord design'd;
Yet since he lives, the gift of life he weighs,
That's time for pray'r, and thus a ground for praise;
From the dark entrails of the whale to thee,
(This new contrivance of a hell to me)
To thee my God I cry'd, my full distress
Pierc'd thy kind ear, and brought my soul redress.
Cast to the deep I fell, by thy command,
Cast in the midst beyond the reach of land;
Then to the midst brought down, the seas abide
Beneath my feet, the seas on ev'ry side;
In storms the billow, and in calms the wave,
Are moving cov'rings to my wand'ring grave;
Forc'd by despair I cry'd; how to my cost
I fled thy presence, Oh for ever lost!
But hope revives my soul, and makes me say,
Yet tow'rds thy temple shall I turn and pray,
Or if I know not here, where Salem lies,

Thy temple's heav'n, and faith has inward eyes.
Alas the waters which my whale surround,
Have thro' my sorr'wing soul a passage found;
And now the dungeon moves, new depths I try,
New thoughts of danger all his paths supply.
The last of Deeps affords the last of dread,
And wraps its funeral weeds around my head:
Now o'er the sand his rollings seem to go
Where the big mountains root their base below;
And now to rocks and clefts their course they take,
Earth's endless bars, too strong for me to break;
Yet from th' Abyss, my God! thy grace divine
Hath call'd him upward, and my life is mine.
Still as I toss'd, I scarce retain'd my breath,
My soul was sick within, and faint to death.
'Twas then I thought of thee, for pity pray'd,
And to thy temple flew the pray'rs I made.
The men whom lying vanity insnares
Forsake thy mercy, that which might be theirs.
But I will pay—my God! my King! receive
The solemn vows my full affection give,
When in thy temple, for a psalm, I sing
Salvation only from my God my king.

Thus ends the prophet, first from Canaan sent,
To let the Gentiles know they must repent:
God hears, and speaks; the Whale at God's command,
Heaves to the light, and casts him forth to land.

With long fatigue, with unexpected ease,
Oppress'd a while, he lies aside the seas,
His eyes tho' glad, in strange astonish'd way
Stare at the golden front of chearful day;
Then slowly rais'd he sees the wonder plain,
And what he pray'd, he wrote to sing again.

The song recorded brings his vow to mind,
He must be thankful, for the Lord was kind;
Strait to the work he shun'd, he flies in haste,
(That seems his vow, or seems a part at least,)
Preaching he comes, and thus denounc'd to all,
Yet forty days and Nineveh shall fall,
Fear seiz'd the Gentiles, Nineveh believes,
All fast with Penitence, and God forgives.

Nor yet of use the prophet's suff'ring fails,
Hell's deep black bosom more than shews the Whales,
But some resemblance brings a type to view,
The place was dark, the time proportion'd too.
A race, the Saviour cries, a sinful race,
Tempts for a sign, the pow'rs of Heav'nly grace,

And let them take the sign, as Jonah lay,
Three days and nights within the fish of prey;
So shall the Son of Man descend below,
Earth's op'ning Entrails shall retain him so.

My soul now seek the song, and find me there,
What Heav'n has shewn thee to repel despair;
See where from Hell she breaks the crumbling ground,
Her hairs stand upright, and they stare around;
Her horrid front, deep-trenching wrinkles trace,
Lean sharp'ning looks deform her livid face;
Bent lie the brows, and at the bend below,
With fire and blood, two wand'ring eye-balls glow;
Fill'd are her arms with num'rous aids to kill,
And God she fancies but the judge of ill;
Oh fair-ey'd Hope! thou see'st the passion nigh,
Daughter of Promise, Oh forbear to fly!
Assurance holds thee, fear would have thee go,
Close thy blue wings and stand thy deadly foe;
The judge of ill is still the Lord of grace,
As such behold him in the Prophet's case;
Cast to be drown'd, devour'd within the sea,
Sunk to the deep, and yet restor'd to day.

Oh love the Lord my soul, whose present care
So rules the world, he punishes to spare.
If heavy grief my downcast heart oppress,
My body danger, or my state distress,
With low submission in thy temper bow,
Like Jonah pray, like Jonah make thy vow,
With hopes of comfort kiss the chast'ning rod,
And shunning mad despair, repose in God;
Then whatsoe'er the Prophet's vow design,
Repentance, Thanks, and Charity be mine.

Solomon

As thro' the Psalms from theme to theme I chang'd,
Methinks like Eve in Paradice I rang'd;
And ev'ry grace of song I seem'd to see,
As the gay pride of ev'ry season, she.
She gently treading all the walks around,
Admir'd the springing beauties of the ground,
The lilly glist'ring with the morning dew,
The rose in red, the violet in blew,
The pink in pale, the bells in purple rows,
And tulips colour'd in a thousand shows:
Then here and there perhaps she pull'd a flow'r
To strew with moss, and paint her leafy bow'r;

And here and there, like her I went along,
Chose a bright strain, and bid it deck my song.

But now the sacred Singer leaves mine eye,
Crown'd as he was, I think he mounts on high;
Ere this Devotion bore his heav'nly psalms,
And now himself bears up his harp and palms.
Go, saint triumphant, leave the changing sight,
So fitted out, you suit the realms of light;
But let thy glorious robe at parting go,
Those realms have robes of more effulgent show;
It flies, it falls, the flutt'ring silk I see,
Thy son has caught it and he sings like thee,
With such election of a theme divine,
And such sweet grace, as conquers all but thine.

Hence, ev'ry writer o'er the fabled streams,
Where frolick fancies sport with idle dreams,
Or round the sight enchanted clouds dispose,
Whence wanton cupids shoot with gilded bows;
A nobler writer, strains more brightly wrought,
Themes more exulted, fill my wond'ring thought:
The parted skies are track'd with flames above,
As love descends to meet ascending love;
The seasons flourish where the spouses meet,
And earth in gardens spreads beneath their feet.
This fresh-bloom prospect in the bosom throngs,
When Solomon begins his song of songs,
Bids the rap'd soul to Lebanon repair,
And lays the scenes of all his action there,
Where as he wrote, and from the bow'r survey'd
The scenting groves, or answ'ring knots he made,
His sacred art the sights of nature brings,
Beyond their use, to figure heav'nly things.

Great son of God! whose gospel pleas'd to throw
Round thy rich glory, veils of earthly show,
Who made the vineyard oft thy church design,
Who made the marriage-feast a type of thine,
Assist my verses which attempt to trace
The shadow'd beauties of celestial grace,
And with illapses of seraphick fire
The work which pleas'd thee once, once more inspire.

Look, or illusion's airy visions draw,
Or now I walk the gardens which I saw,
Where silver waters feed a flow'ring spring,
And winds salute it with a balmy wing.
There on a bank, whose shades directly rise
To screen the sun, and not exclude the skies,
There sits the sacred church; methinks I view

The spouse's aspect and her ensigns too.
Her face has features where the virtues reign,
Her hands the book of sacred love contain,
A light (truth's emblem) on her bosom shines
And at her side the meekest lamb reclines:
And oft on heav'nly lectures in the book,
And oft on heav'n itself, she cast a look;
Sweet, humble, fervent zeal that works within
At length bursts forth, and raptures thus begin.

Let Him, that Him my soul adores above,
In close communions breath his holy love;
For these bless'd words his pleasing lips impart,
Beyond all cordials, chear the fainting heart.
As rich and sweet, the precious ointments stream,
So rich thy graces flow, so sweet thy name
Diffuses sacred joy; tis hence we find
Affection rais'd in ev'ry virgin mind;
For this we come, the daughters here and I,
Still draw we forward, and behold I fly,
I fly through mercy, when my king invites,
To tread his chambers of sincere delights;
There, join'd by mystick union, I rejoice,
Exalt my temper, and enlarge my voice,
And celebrate thy joys, supremely more
Than earthly bliss; thus upright hearts adore.
Nor you ye maids, who breath of Salem's air,
Nor you refuse that I conduct you there;
Tho' clouding darkness hath eclips'd my face,
Dark as I am, I shine with beams of grace,
As the black tents, where Ishmael's line abides,
With glitt'ring trophies dress their inward sides;
Or as thy curtains, Solomon, are seen,
Whose plaits conceal a golden throne within.
'Twere wrong to judge me by the carnal sight,
And yet my visage was by nature white,
But fiery suns which persecute the meek,
Found me abroad, and scorch'd my rosy cheek.
The world, my brethren, they were angry grown,
They made me dress a vineyard not my own,
Among their rites, (their vines) I learn'd to dwell,
And in the mean employ my beauty fell;
By frailty lost, I gave my labour o'er
And my own vineyard grew deform'd the more.
Behold I turn, O say my soul's desire,
Where do'st thou feed thy flock and where retire
To rest that flock, when noon-tide heats arise?
Shepherd of Israel, teach my dubious eyes
To guide me right, for why shou'd thine abide
Where wand'ring shepherds turn their flocks aside?

So spake the church and sigh'd, a purple light
Sprung forth, the Godhead stood reveal'd to sight,
And heav'n and nature smil'd; as white as snow
His seamless vesture loosely fell below;
Sedate and pleas'd he nodded, round his head
The pointed glory shook, and thus he said:
If thou the loveliest of the beauteous kind,
If thou canst want thy shepherd's walk to find,
Go by the foot-steps where my flocks have trod,
My saints obedient to the laws of God,
Go where their tents my teaching servants rear,
And feed the kids, thy young believers there.
Shou'd thus my flocks increase, my fair delight,
I view their numbers, and compare the sight
To Pharaoh's Horses, when they take the field,
Beat plains to dust, and make the nations yield.
With rows of gems, thy comely cheeks I deck,
And chains of pendant gold o'erflow thy neck,
For so like gems the riches of my grace,
And so descending glory, chears thy face:
Gay bridal robes a flow'ring silver strows,
Bright gold engrailing on the border glows.

He spake, the spouse admiring heard the sound,
Then meekly bending on the sacred ground,
She cries, Oh present to my ravish'd breast,
This sweet communion is an inward feast;
There sits the king, while all around our heads,
His grace, my Spikenard, pleasing odours sheds;
About my soul his holy comfort flies,
So closely treasur'd in the bosom lies
The bundled myrrhe, so sweet the scented gale
Breaths all En-gedi's aromatick vale.
Now says the king, my love, I see thee fair,
Thine eyes for mildness with the dove's compare.

No, thou, belov'd, art fair, the church replies,
(Since all my beauties but from thee arise,)
All fair, all pleasant, these communions shew
Thy councels pleasant, and thy comforts so.
And as at marriage feasts they strow the flow'rs,
With nuptial chaplets hang the summer bow'rs,
And make the rooms of smelling cedars fine,
Where the fond bridegroom and the bride recline;
I dress my soul, with such exceeding care,
With such, with more, to court thy presence there.

Well hast thou prais'd, he says; the Sharon rose
Through flow'ry fields a pleasing odour throws,
The valley-lillies ravish'd sense regale,
And with pure whiteness paint their humble vale;

Such names of sweetness are thy lover's due,
And thou my love, be thou a lilly too,
A lilly set in thorns; for all I see,
All other daughters are as thorns to thee.

Then she; the trees that pleasing apples yield,
Surpass the barren trees that cloath the field,
So you surpass the sons with worth divine,
So shade, and fruit as well as shade, is thine.
I sat me down, and saw thy branches spread,
And green protection flourish o'er my head,
I saw thy fruit, the soul's celestial food,
I pull'd, I tasted, and I found it good.
Hence in the spirit to the blissful seats,
Where love, to feast, mysteriously retreats,
He led me forth; I saw the banner rear,
And love was pencil'd for the motto there.
Prophets and teachers, in your care combine,
Stay me with apples, comfort me with wine,
The cordial promises of joys above,
For hope deferr'd has made me sick with love.
Ah! while my tongue reveals my fond desire,
His hands support me, least my life expire;
As round a child the parent's arms are plac'd,
This holds the head, and that enfolds the waist.

Here ceas'd the church, and lean'd her languid head
Bent down with joy, when thus the lover said:
Behold, ye daughters of the realm of peace,
She sleeps, at least her thoughts of sorrow cease.
Now, by the bounding roes, the skipping fawns,
Near the cool brooks, or o'er the grassy lawns,
By all the tender innocents that rove,
Your hourly charges in my sacred grove,
Guard the dear charge from each approach of ill,
I wou'd not have her wake, but when she will.

So rest the church and spouse, my verses so
Appear to languish with the flames you shew,
And pausing rest; but not the pause be long,
For still thy Solomon pursues the song.
Then keep the place in view; let sweets more rare
Than earth produces, fill the purpled air;
Let something solemn overspread the green
Which seems to tell us, here the Lord has been:
But let the virgin still in prospect shine,
And other strains of hers, enliven mine.
She wakes, she rises; bid the whisp'ring breeze
More softly whisper in the waving trees,
Or fall with silent awe; bid all around,
Before the church's voice, abate their sound,

While thus her shadowy strains attempt to shew
A future advent of the spouse below.

Hark! my beloved's voice! behold him too!
Behold him coming in the distant view,
No clamb'ring mountains make my lover stay,
(For what are mountains, in a lover's way?)
Leaping he comes, how like the nimble roe
He runs the paths his prophets us'd to shew!
And now he looks from yon partition wall,
Built till he comes—'tis only then to fall,
And now he's nearer in the promise seen,
Too faint the sight—tis with a glass between;
From hence I hear him as a lover speak,
Who near a window, calls a fair to wake.

Attend ye virgins, while the words that trace
An opening spring, design the day of grace.
Hark! or I dream, or else I hear him say,
Arise my love, my fair one, come away,
For now the tempests of thy winter end,
Thick rains no more in heavy drops descend,
Sweet painted flow'rs their silken leaves unclose,
And dress the face of earth with vari'd shows;
In the green wood the singing birds renew
Their chirping notes, the silver turtles coo:
The trees that yield the fig, already shoot,
And knit their blossoms for their early fruit;
With fragrant scents the vines refresh the day,
Arise my love, my fair one come away.
O come my dove, forsake thy close retreat,
For close in safety hast thou fix'd thy seat,
As fearful pidgeons in dark clefts abide,
And safe the clefts their tender charges hide.
Now let thy looks with modest guise appear,
Now let thy voice salute my longing ear,
For in thy looks an humble mind I see,
Prayer forms thy voice, and both are sweet to me.
To save the bloomings of my vineyard, haste,
Which foxes, (false deluding teachers) waste;
Watch well their haunts, and catch the foxes there,
Our grapes are tender and demand the care.
Thus speaks my love: surprizing love divine!
I thus am his, he thus for ever mine.
And 'till he comes, I find a presence still,
Where souls attentive serve his holy will,
Where down in vales unspotted lillies grow,
White types of innocence, in humble show.
O 'till the spicy breath of heav'nly day,
Till all thy shadows fleet before thy ray,
Turn my beloved with thy comforts here,

Turn in thy promise, in thy grace appear,
Nor let such swiftness in the roes be shown
To save themselves, as thou to chear thine own;
Turn like the nimble harts that lightly bound
Before the stretches of the fleetest hound,
Skim the plain chace of lofty Bether's head,
And make the mountain wonder if they tread.

But long expectance of a bliss delay'd
Breeds anxious doubt, and tempts the sacred maid;
Then mists arising strait repel the light,
The colour'd garden lies disguis'd with night,
A pale-horn'd crescent leads a glimm'ring throng,
And groans of absence jarr within the song.

By night, she cries, a night which blots the mind,
I seek the lover, whom I fail to find;
When on my couch compos'd to thought I lie,
I search, and vainly search with reason's eye;
Rise fondly rise, thy present search give o'er
And ask if others know thy lover more.
Dark as it is, I rise, the moon that shines,
Shows by the gleam, the city's outward lines,
I range the wand'ring road, the winding street,
And ask, but ask in vain, of all I meet,
'Till, toil'd with ev'ry disappointing place
My steps the guardians of the temple trace,
Whom thus my wish accosts, ye sacred guides,
Ye prophets, tell me where my love resides?
'Twas well I question'd, scarce I pass'd them by,
Ere my rais'd soul perceives my lover nigh:
And have I found thee, found my joy divine?
How fast I'll hold thee, 'till I make thee mine.
My mother waits thee, thither thou repair,
Long waiting Israel wants thy presence there.
The lover smiles to see the virgin's pain,
The mists roll off, and quit the flow'ry plain.

Yes, here I come, he says, thy sorrow cease,
And guard her, daughters of the realms of peace,
By all the bounding roes and skipping fawns,
Near the cool brooks, or o'er the grassy lawns,
By all the tender innocents that rove,
Your hourly charges, in my sacred grove;
Guard the dear charge from each approach of ill,
I'll have her feel my comforts, while she will.

Here hand in hand with chearful heart they go,
When wand'ring Salem sees the solemn show,
Dreams the rich pomp of Solomon again,
And thus her daughters sing the approaching scene.

Who from the desart, where the waving clouds
High Sinai pierces, comes involv'd with crowds?
For Sion's hill her sober pace she bends,
As grateful incense from the Dome ascends.
It seems the sweets from all Arabia shed,
Curl at her side, and hover o'er her head.
For her the king prepares a bed of state,
Round the rich bed her guards in order wait,
All mystick Israel's sons, 'tis there they quell
The foes within, the foes without repel.
The guard his ministry, their swords of fight
His sacred laws, her present state of night.
He forms a chariot too to bring her there,
Not the carv'd frame of Solomon's so fair;
Sweet smells the chariot as the temple stood,
The fragrant cedar lent them both the wood,
High wreaths of silver'd columns prop the door,
Fine gold entrail'd, adorns the figur'd floor,
Deep fringing purple hangs the roof above,
And silk embroid'ry paints the midst with love.

Go forth ye daughters, Sion's daughters go,
A greater Solomon exalts the show,
If crown'd with gold, and by the queen bestow'd,
To grace his nuptials, Jacob's monarch rode;
A crown of glory from the king divine,
To grace these nuptials, makes the Saviour shine;
While the bless'd pair, express'd in emblem ride,
Messiah Solomon, his church the bride.

Ye kind attendants who with wond'ring eyes
Saw the grand entry, what you said suffice,
You sung the lover with a loud acclaim,
The lover's fondness longs to sing the dame.
He speaks, admiring nature stands around
And learns new musick, while it hears the sound.

Behold, my love, how fair thy beauties show,
Behold how more, how most extremely so!
How still to me thy constant eyes incline,
I see the turtle's when I gaze on thine,
Sweet through the lids they shine with modest care,
And sweet and modest is a virgin's air.
How bright thy locks! how well their number paints
The great assemblies of my lovely saints!
So bright the kids, so numerously fed,
Graze the green top of lofty Gilead's head;
All Gilead's head a fleecy whiteness clouds,
And the rich master glorys in the crowds.

How pure thy teeth! for equal order made,
Each answ'ring each, whilst all the publick aid,
These lovely graces in my church I find,
This candour, order, and accorded mind:
Thus when the season bids the shepherd lave
His sheep new shorn, within the chrystal wave,
Wash'd they return, in such unsully'd white,
Thus march by pairs, and in the flock unite.
How please thy lips adorn'd with native red!
Art vainly mocks them in the scarlet thread!
But if they part, what musick wafts the air!
So sweet thy praises, and so soft thy Prayer.
If through thy loosen'd curls with honest shame
Thy lovely temples fine complexion flame,
Whatever crimson Granate blossoms show,
'Twas never theirs, so much to please, and glow.
But what's thy neck, the polish'd form I see!
Whose Iv'ry strength supports thine eyes to me;
Fair type of firmness when my saints aspire,
The sacred confidence that lifts desire,
As David's turret on the stately frame
Upheld its thousand conqu'ring shields of fame.
And what thy breasts! they still demand my lays,
What image wakes to charm me whilst I gaze?
Two lovely mountains each exactly round,
Two lovely mountains with the lilly crown'd,
While two twin roes, and each on either bred,
Feed in the lillies of the mountain's head.
Let this resemblance, spotless virtues show,
And in such lillies feed my young below.
But now farewell 'till night's dark shades decay,
Farewel my virgin, 'till the break of day,
Swift for the hills of spice and gums I fly,
To breath such sweets as scent a purer sky,
Yet as I leave thee, still above compare,
My Love, my spotless, still I find thee fair.

Here rest celestial maid, for if he go,
Nor will he part, nor is the promise slow,
Nor slow my fancy move; dispel the shade,
Charm forth the morning and relieve the maid.
Arise fair sun, the church attends to see
The sun of righteousness arise in thee;
Arise fair Sun, and bid the church adore,
'Tis then he'll court her, whom he prais'd before.
As thus I sing, it shines, there seems a sound
Of plumes in air, and feet upon the ground;
I see their meeting, see the flow'ry scene
And hear the mystick love pursu'd again.

Now to the mount whose spice perfumes the day,

'Tis I invite thee, come my spouse away,
Come, leave thy Lebanon, is ought we see
In all thy Lebanon, compared to me?
Nor tow'rd thy Canaan turn with wishful sight,
From Hermon's, Shenir's, and Amana's height;
There dwells the leopard, there assaults the bear,
This world has ills, and such may find thee there.

My spouse, my sister, O thy wond'rous art,
Which through my bosom drew my ravish'd heart!
Won by one eye, my ravish'd heart is gone,
For all thy seeing guides consent as one,
Drawn by one chain which round thy body plies,
For all thy members one bless'd union ties.
My spouse, my sister, O the charm to please,
When love repaid, returns my bosom ease!
Strongly thy love, and strongly wines restore,
But wines must yield, thy love enflames me more.
Sweetly thine ointments, (all thy virtues) smell,
Not altar spices please thy king so well.
How soft thy doctrine on thy lips resides!
From those two combs the dropping honey glides,
All pure without as all within sincere,
Beneath thy tongue—I find it honey there.
Ah while thy graces thus around thee shine,
The charms of Lebanon must yield to thine!
His spring, his garden, ev'ry scented tree,
My spouse, my sister, all I find in thee.
Thee for myself I fence, I shut, I seal,
Mysterious spring, mysterious garden, hail!
A spring, a font, where heav'nly waters flow,
A grove, a garden, where the graces grow.
There rise my fruits, my cyprus, and my firr,
My saffron, spikenard, Cinnamon and Myrrhe;
Perpetual fountains for their use abound,
And streams of favour feed the living ground.

Scarce spake the Christ, when thus the church replies
(And spread her arms where e'er the spirit flies.)
Ye cooling northern gales, who freshly shake
My balmy reeds, ye northern gales awake.
And thou the regent of the southern sky,
O soft inspiring o'er my garden fly,
Unlock and waft my sweets, that ev'ry grace
In all its heav'nly life regale the place.
If thus a paradice thy garden prove,
'Twere best prepar'd to entertain my love,
And that the pleasing fruits may please the more,
O think my proffer, was thy gift before.

At this, the Saviour cries, behold me near,

My spouse, my sister, O behold me here,
To gather fruits, I come at thy request,
And pleas'd my soul accepts the solemn feast;
I gather myrrhe with spice to scent the treat,
My virgin-honey with the combs I eat,
I drink my sweet'ning milk, my lively wine,
(These words of pleasure mean thy gifts divine)
To share my bliss, my good elect I call,
The church (my garden) must include them all;
Now sit and banquet, now belov'd you see
What gifts I love, and prove these fruits with me;
O might this sweet communion ever last!
But with the sun the sweet communion past,
The Saviour parts, and on oblivion's breast
Benumb'd and slumb'ring lies the church to rest,
Pass the sweet allies while the dusk abides,
Seek the fair lodge in which the maid resides,
Then, fancy, seek the maid, at night again
The Christ will come, but comes, alas in vain.

I sleep, she says, and yet my heart awakes,
(There's still some feeling while the lover speaks)
With what fond fervour from without he cries!
Arise my love, my undefil'd arise,
My dove, my sister, cold the dews alight,
And fill my tresses with the drops of night;
Alas I'm all unrob'd, I wash'd my feet,
I tasted slumber, and I find it sweet.

As thus my words refuse, he slips his hands
Where the clos'd latch my cruel door commands.
What, tho' deny'd, so persevering kind!
Who long denies a persevering mind?
From my wak'd soul my slothful temper flies,
My bowels yearn, I rise, my love, I rise,
I find the latch thy fingers touch'd before,
Thy smelling myrrhe comes dropping off the door.
Now where's my love?—what! hast thou left the place?
O, to my soul, repeat thy words of grace,
Speak in the dark, my love; I seek thee round
And vainly seek thee 'till thou wilt be found.
What no return? I own my folly past,
I lay too listless; speak my love at last.
The guards have found me—are ye guards indeed,
Who smite the sad, who make the feeble bleed?
Dividing teachers these; who wrong my name,
Rend my long veil, and cast me bare to shame.
But you, ye daughters of the realm of rest,
If ever pity mov'd a virgin breast,
Tell my belov'd how languishing I lie,
How love has brought me near the point to dye.

And what belov'd is this you wou'd have found,
Say Salem's daughters, as they flock'd around?
What wond'rous thing? what charm beyond compare?
Say what's thy lover, fairest o'er the fair?
His face is white and ruddy, she replies,
So mercy join'd to justice, tempers dyes;
His lofty stature, where a Myriad shine,
O'ertops, and speaks a majesty divine.
Fair honour crowns his head, the raven-black
In bushy curlings flows adown his back.
Sparkling his eyes, with full proportion plac'd,
White like the milk, and with a mildness grac'd;
As the sweet doves, when e'er they fondly play
By running waters in a glitt'ring day.
Within his breath, what pleasing sweetness grows!
'Tis spice exhal'd, and mingl'd on the rose.
Within his words, what grace with goodness meets!
So beds of lillies drop with balmy sweets.
What rings of eastern price his finger hold!
Gold decks the fingers, Beryl decks the gold!
His Iv'ry shape adorns a costly vest,
Work paints the skirts, and gems inrich the breast;
His limbs beneath, his shining sandals case
Like marble columns on a golden base.

Nor boasts that mountain, where the cedar tree
Perfumes our realm, such num'rous sweets as he.
O lovely all! what cou'd my king require
To make his presence more the world's desire?
And now ye maids if such a friend you know,
'Tis such my longings look to find below.

While thus her friend, the spouse's Anthems sing,
Deck'd with the Thummim, crown'd a sacred king,
The Daughter's hearts, the fine description drew,
And that which rais'd their wonder, ask'd their view.

Then where, they cry, thou fairest o'er the fair,
Where goes thy lover, tell the virgins where?
What flow'ring walks invite his steps aside?
We'll help to seek him, let those walks be try'd.

The spouse revolving here the grand descent,
'Twas that he promis'd, there, she cries, he went,
He keeps a garden where the spices breath,
Its bow'ring borders kiss the vale beneath,
'Tis there he gathers lillies, there he dwells,
And binds his flow'rets to unite their smells.
O 'tis my height of love, that I am his!
O he is mine, and that's my height of bliss!

Descend my virgins, well I know the place,
He feeds in lillies, that's a spotless race.

At dawning day, the bridegroom leaves a bow'r,
And here he waters, there he props a flow'r,
When the kind damsel, spring of heav'nly flame,
With Salem's daughters to the garden came.
Then thus his love the bridegroom's words repeat
(The smelling borders lent them both a seat.)
O great as Tirzah! 'twas a regal place,
O fair as Salem! 'tis the realm of peace,
Whose aspect, awful to the wond'ring eye,
Appears like armies when the banners fly;
O turn my sister, O my beauteous bride,
Thy face o'ercomes me, turn that face aside,
How bright thy locks, how well their number paints
The great assemblies of my lovely saints,
So bright the kids, so numerously fed,
Graze the green wealth of lofty Gilead's head.
How pure thy teeth! for equal order made,
Each answ'ring each, while all the publick aid;
As when the season bids the shepherd lave
His sheep new shorn within the silver wave,
Wash'd they return in such unsully'd white,
So march by pairs, and in the flock unite.
How sweet thy temples! not pomegranates know
With equal modest look to please and glow.
If Solomon his life of pleasure leads,
With wives in numbers, and unnumbered maids,
In other paths, my life of pleasure shewn,
Admits my love, my undefil'd alone;
Thy mother Israel, she the dame who bore
Her choice, my dove, my spotless owns no more;
The Gentile queens at thy appearance cry,
Hail queen of nations! hail, the maids reply,
And thus they sing thy praise: what heav'nly dame
Springs like the morning with a purple flame?
What rises like the morn with silver light?
What like the sun assists the world with sight?
Yet awful still, tho' thus serenely kind,
Like hosts with ensigns rattling in the wind.
I grant I left thy sight, I seem'd to go,
But was I absent when you fancy'd so?
Down to my garden, all my planted vale,
Where nuts their ground in underwood conceal,
Where blow pomegranates, there I went to see
What knitting blossoms white the bearing tree,
View the green buds, recall the wand'ring shoots,
Smell my gay flow'rets, taste my flavour'd fruits,
Raise the curl'd vine, refresh the spicy beds,
And joy for ev'ry grace my garden sheds.

The Saviour here, and here the church arise,
And am I thus respected, thus she cries!
I mount for heav'n transported on the winds,
My flying chariot's drawn by willing minds.

As rap'd with comfort thus the maid withdrew,
The waiting daughters wonder'd where she flew,
And O! return, they cry, for thee we burn,
O maid of Salem, Salem's self return.
And what's in Salem's maid we covet so?
Here all ye nations—'tis your bliss below;
That glorious vision by the patriarch seen,
When sky-born beauties march'd the scented green,
There the met saints, and meeting angels came,
Two lamps of God, Mahanaim was the name.

Again the maid reviews her sacred ground,
Solemn she sits, the damsels sing around.

O princes daughter! how with shining show
Thy golden shoes prepare thy feet below!
How firm thy joints! what temple-work can be
With all its gems and art preferr'd to thee?
In thee, to feed thy lover's faithful race,
Still flow the riches of abounding grace,
Pure, large, refreshing, as the waters fall
From the carv'd navels of the cistern-wall.
In thee the lover finds his race divine,
You teem with numbers, they with virtues shine;
So wheat with lillies, if their heaps unite,
The wheat's unnumb'red and the lillies white;
Like tender roes thy breasts appear above,
Two types of innocence and twins of love.
Like Iv'ry turrets seems thy neck to rear,
O sacred emblem, upright, firm and fair!
As Heshbon pools, which with a silver state
Diffuse their waters at their city gate,
For ever so thy virgin eyes remain,
So clear within, and so without serene.
As thro' sweet Firr the royal turret shews,
Whence Lebanon surveys a realm of foes,
So thro' thy lovely curls appear thy face
To watch thy foes, and guard thy faithful race.
The richest colours flow'ry Carmel wears,
Red fillets cross'd with purple braid thy hairs;
Yet not more strictly these thy locks restrain
Than thou thy king with strong affections chain,
When from his palace he enjoys thy sight,
O love, O beauty, form'd for all delight!
Strait is thy goodly stature, firm, and high,

As palms aspiring in the brighter sky;
Thy breasts the cluster, (if those breasts we view
As late for beauty, now for profit too.)
Woo'd to thine arms, those arms that oft extend
In the kind posture of a waiting friend,
Each maid of Salem cries, I'll mount the tree,
Hold the broad branches, and depend on thee.
O more than grapes, thy fruit delights the maids,
Thy pleasing breath excels the Citron shades,
Thy mouth exceeds rich wine, the words that go
From those sweet lips, with more refreshment flow,
Their pow'rful graces slumb'ring souls awake
And cause the dead that hear thy voice to speak.

This anthem sung, the glorious spouse arose,
Yet thus instructs the daughters ere she goes.
If ought, my damsels, in the spouse ye find
Deserving praises, think the lover kind:
To my belov'd these marriage robes I owe,
I'm his desire, and he wou'd have it so.

Scarce spake the spouse, but see the lover near,
Her humble temper brought the Presence here;
Then rais'd by grace, and strongly warm'd by love,
No second Languor lets her Lord remove,
She flies to meet him, zeal supplies the wings,
And thus her haste to work his will she sings;
Come my beloved, to the fields repair,
Come where another spot demands our care,
There in the village we'll to rest recline,
Mean as it is I try to make it thine.
When the first rays their chearing crimson shed,
We'll rise betimes to see the Vineyard spread,
See Vines luxuriant verdur'd leaves display,
Supporting Tendrils curling all the way,
See young unpurpled Grapes in clusters grow,
And smell Pomegranate blossoms as they blow;
There will I give my loves, employ my care,
And as my labours thrive, approve me there.
Scarce have we pass'd my gate, the scent we meet;
My covering Jessamines diffuse a sweet,
My spicy flow'rets mingled as they fly,
With doubling odours crowd a balmy sky.
Now all the fruits which crown the season view,
These nearer Fruits are old, and those are new,
And these, and all of ev'ry loaded tree,
My love I gather and reserve for thee.
If then thy spouse's labour please thee well,
Oh! like my brethren with thy Sister dwell;
No blameless maid, whose fond caresses meet
An Infant-brother in the publick street,

Clings to its lips with less reserve than I
Wou'd hang on thine where'er I found thee nigh:
No shame wou'd make me from thy side remove,
No danger make me not confess thy love.
Strait to my Mother's house, thine Israel she,
(And thou my Monarch wou'dst arrive with me,)
'Tis there I'd lead thee, where I mean to stay,
'Till thou, by her, instruct my Soul to pray;
There shal't thou prove my virtues, drink my Wine,
And feel my joy to find me wholly thine.
Oh! while my soul were sick thro' fond desire,
Thine hands shou'd hold me least my life expire;
As round a child the Parent's arms are plac'd,
This holds the head, and that enfolds the waist.

So cast thy cares on me, the lover cry'd,
Lean to my bosom, lean my lovely Bride,
And now ye daughters of the realm of bliss,
Let nothing discompose a love like this;
But guard her rest from each approach of ill,
I caus'd her Languor, guard her while she will.

Here pause the lines, but soon the lines renew,
Once more the pair celestial come to view;
Ah! seek them once, my ravish'd fancy, more,
And then thy songs of Solomon are o'er:
By yon green bank pursue their orb of light,
The Sun shines out, but shines not half so bright.
See Salem's maids in white attend the King,
They greet the Spouses—hark to what they sing.

Who from the Desart, where the wand'ring clouds
High Sinai pierces, comes involv'd with crowds?
'Tis she, the Spouse, Oh! favour'd o'er the rest!
Who walks reclin'd by such a lover's breast.

The Spouse rejoicing heard the kind salute,
And thus address'd him—all the rest were mute.
Beneath the law, our goodly parent tree,
I went my much belov'd in search of thee,
For thee, like one in pangs of travail strove,
Hence, none may wonder if I gain thy love.
As seals their pictures to the wax impart,
So let my picture stamp thy gentle heart,
As fix'd the Signets on our hands remain,
So fix me thine, and ne'er to part again;
For love is strong as Death, whene'er they strike,
Alike imperious, vainly check'd alike;
But dread to loose, love mix'd with jealous dread!
As soon the marble Tomb resign the dead.
Its fatal arrows fiery-pointed fall,

The fire intense, and thine the most of all;
To slack the points no chilling floods are found,
Nay shou'd afflictions roll like floods around,
Were wealth of nations offer'd, all wou'd prove
Too small a danger, or a price for love.
If then with love this world of worth agree,
With soft regard our little Sister see,
How far unapt as yet, like maids that own
No Breasts at all, or Breasts but hardly grown,
Her part of Proselyte is scarce a part,
Too much a Gentile at her erring heart,
Her day draws nearer, what have we to do,
Least she be ask'd, and prove unworthy too?

Despair not Spouse, he cries, we'll find the means,
Her good beginnings ask the greater pains.
Let her but stand, she thrives; a wall too low
Is not rejected for the standing so;
What falls is only lost, we'll build her high,
'Till the rich palace glitters in the sky.
The Door that's weak, (what need we spare the cost?)
If tis a door, we need not think it lost;
The Leaves she brings us, if those Leaves be good,
We'll close in Cedar's uncorrupting wood.

Rap'd with the news, the spouse converts her eyes,
And Oh! companions, to the maids she cries;
What joys are ours to hail the nuptial day
Which calls our Sister?—Hark I hear her say,
Yes I'm a wall; lo! she that boasted none,
Now boasts of Breasts unmeasurably grown,
Large tow'ry buildings, where securely rest
A thousand thousand of my lovers guests;
The vast increase affords his heart delight,
And I find favour in his Heav'nly sight.
The Lover here, to make her rapture last,
Thus adds assurance to the promise past.

A spacious Vineyard in Baal-Hamon vale,
The vintage set, by Solomon, to sale,
His keepers took; and ev'ry keeper paid
A thousand Purses for the gains he made.
And I've a vintage too; his vintage bleeds
A large increase, but my return exceeds.
Let Solomon receive his keepers pay,
He gains his thousand, their two hundred they;
Mine is mine own, 'tis in my presence still,
And shall increase the more, the more she will.
My love my Vineyard, Oh the future shoots,
Which fill my garden rows with sacred fruits!
I saw the list'ning maids attend thy voice,

And in their list'ning saw their eyes rejoice,
A due success thy words of comfort met,
Now turn to me—'tis I wou'd hear thee yet.
Say dove and spotless, for I must away,
Say Spouse and Sister, all you wish to say.
He spake, the place was bright with lambent fire,
(But what is brightness if the Christ retire?)
Gold bord'ring purple mark'd his road in air,
And kneeling all, the Spouse address'd the pray'r.

Desire of nations! if thou must be gone,
Accept our wishes, all compriz'd in one;
We wait thine advent, Oh we long to see,
I and my Sister, both as one in thee.
Then leave thy Heav'n, and come and dwell below,
Why said I leave?—'tis Heav'n where ere you go.
Haste my belov'd, thy promise haste to crown,
The form thou'lt honour waits thy coming down,
Nor let such swiftness in the Roes be shewn
To save themselves, as thine to save thine own.
Haste like the nimblest Harts, that lightly bound
Before the stretches of the swiftest Hound,
With reaching feet devour a level way,
Across their backs their branching antlers lay,
In the cool dews their bending body ply,
And brush the spicy mountains as they fly.

Moses

To grace those lines wch next appear to sight,
The Pencil shone with more abated light,
Yet still ye pencil shone, ye lines were fair,
& awfull Moses stands recorded there.
Lett his repleat with flames & praise divine
Lett his the first-rememberd Song be mine.
Then rise my thought, & in thy Prophet find
What Joy shoud warm thee for ye work designd.
To that great act which raisd his heart repair,
& find a portion of his Spirit there.

A Nation helpless & unarmd I view,
Whom strong revengefull troops of warr pursue,
Seas Stop their flight, their camp must prove their grave.
Ah what can Save them? God alone can save.
Gods wondrous voice proclaims his high command,
He bids their Leader wave the sacred wand,
& where the billows flowd they flow no more,
A road lyes naked & they march it o're.
Safe may the Sons of Jacob travell through,

But why will Hardend Ægypt venture too?
Vain in thy rage to think the waters flee,
& rise like walls on either hand for thee.
The night comes on the Season for surprize,
Yet fear not Israel God directs thine eyes,
A fiery cloud I see thine Angel ride,
His Chariot is thy light & he thy guide.
The day comes on & half thy succours fail,
Yet fear not Israel God will still prevail,
I see thine Angel from before thee go,
To make the wheeles of ventrous Ægypt slow,
His rolling cloud inwraps its beams of light,
& what supplyd thy day prolongs their night.
At length the dangers of the deep are run,
The Further brink is past, the bank is won,
The Leader turns to view the foes behind,
Then waves his solemn wand within the wind.
O Nation freed by wonders cease thy fear,
& stand & see the Lords salvation here.

Ye tempests now from ev'ry corner fly,
& wildly rage in all my fancyd Sky.
Roll on ye waters as ye rolld before,
Ye billows of my fancyd ocean roar,
Dash high, ride foaming, mingle all ye main.
Tis don—& Pharaoh cant afflict again.
The work the wondrous work of Freedomes don,
The winds abate, the clouds restore ye Sun,
The wreck appears, the threatning army drownd
Floats ore ye waves to strow the Sandy ground.

Then Place thy Moses near the calming flood,
Majestically mild, serenely good.
Lett Meekness (Lovely virtue) gently Stream
Around his visage like a lambent flame.
Lett gratefull Sentiments, lett Sense of love,
Lett holy zeal within his bosome move.
& while his People gaze ye watry plain,
& fears last touches like to doubt remain,
While bright astonishment that seems to raise
A questioning belief, is fond to praise,
Be thus the rapture in the Prophets breast,
Be thus the thankes for freedome gaind expresst.

Ile sing to God, Ile Sing ye songs of praise
To God triumphant in his wondrous ways,
To God whose glorys in the Seas excell,
Where the proud horse & prouder rider fell.

The Lord in mercy kind in Justice strong

Is now my strength, this Strength be now my song,
This sure salvation, (such he proves to me
from danger rescu'd & from bondage free).
The Lords my God & Ile prepare his seat,
My Fathers God & Ile proclaim him great,
Him Lord of Battles, him renownd in name,
Him ever faithfull, evermore the same.

His gracious aids avenge his peoples thrall,
They make the pride of boasting Pharaoh fall.
Within the Seas his stately Chariots ly,
Within the Seas his chosen Captains dy.
The rolling deeps have coverd o're the foe,
They sunk like stones they Swiftly sunk below.
There O my God thine hand confessd thy care,
Thine hand was glorious in thy power there,
It broke their troops unequall for the fight
In all the greatness of excelling might.
Thy wrath Sent forward on ye raging Stream,
Swift sure & Sudden their destruction came,
They fell as stubble burns, while driving skys
Provoke & whirl a flame & ruin fly's.

When blasts dispatchd with wonderfull intent
On soveraign orders from thy nostrills went,
For our accounts the waters were affraid,
Perceivd thy presence & together fled,
In heaps uprightly placd they learnd to stand,
like banks of Christall by ye paths of sand.
Then fondly flushd with hope, & swelld with pride,
& filld with rage, the foe prophanely cryd,
Secure of conquest Ile pursue their way,
Ile overtake them, Ile divide the prey,
My lust I'le Satisfy, mine anger cloy,
My sword Ile brandish, & their name destroy.
How wildly threats their anger: hark above
New blasts of wind on new commission move,
To loose the fetters that confind the main,
& make its mighty waters rage again,
Then overwhelmd with irresistless Sway
They Sunk like lead they sunk beneath the Sea.

O who like thee thou dreaded Lord of Host
Among the Gods whom all the nations boast
Such acts of wonder & of Strength displays,
O Great! O Glorious in thine holy ways!
Deserving praise, & that thy praise appear
In Signs of reverence & Sence of fear.
With Justice armd thou stretcht thy powrfull hand,
& earth between its gaping Jaws of land,
Receivd its waters of the parted main,

& swallowd up the dark Ægyptian train.
With mercy rising on the weaker Side,
Thy self became the rescud peoples guide,
& in thy strength they past th' amazing road,
To reach thine holy mount thy blessd abode.

What thou hast don the neighb'ring realms shall hear,
& feel the strange report excite their fear.
What thou hast don shall Edoms Dukes amaze,
& make dispair on Palestina Seize.
Shall make the warlike Sons of Moab Shake,
& all the melting hearts of Canaan weak.
In heavy damps diffusd on ev'ry breast
Shall cold distrust & hopeless Terrour rest.
The matchless greatness which thine hand has shown,
Shall keep their kingdomes as unmovd as stone,
While Jordan Stops above & failes below,
& all thy flock across the Channel go.
Thus on thy mercys silver-shining wing
Through seas & streams thou wilt ye nation bring,
& as the rooted trees securely stand,
So firmly plant it in the promisd land,
Where for thy self thou wilt a place prepare,
& after-ages will thine altar rear.
There reign victorious in thy Sacred Seat,
O Lord for ever & for ever great.

Look where the Tyrant was but lately seen,
The Seas gave backward & he venturd in,
In yonder gulph with haughty pomp he showd,
Here marchd his horsemen, there his chariots rode;
& when our God restord the floods again,
Ah vainly strong they perishd in the main.
But Israel went a dry surprizing way,
Made safe by miracles amidst ye sea.

Here ceasd the Song, tho' not ye Prophets Joy,
Which others hands & others tongues employ.
For still the lays with warmth divine expresst
Inflamd his hearers to their inmost breast.
Then Miriams notes the Chorus sweetly raise,
& Miriams timbrel gives new life to praise.
The moving sounds, like Soft delicious wind
That breathd from Paradise, a passage find,
Shed Sympathys for Odours as they rove,
& fan the risings of enkindled love.
Ore all ye crowd the thought inspiring flew,
The women followd with their timbrells too,
& thus from Moses where his strains arose,
They catchd a rapture to perform the close.

We'le sing to God, we'le sing ye songs of praise
To God triumphant in his wondrous ways,
To God whose glorys in ye Seas excell,
Where ye proud horse & prouder rider fell.

Thus Israel rapturd wth ye pleasing thought
Of Freedome wishd & wonderfully gott,
Made chearfull thanks from evry bank rebound,
Expressd by songs, improvd in Joy by sound.

O Sacred Moses, each infusing line
That movd their gratitude was part of thine,
& still the Christians in thy numbers view,
The type of Baptism & of Heaven too.
So Soules from water rise to Grace below:
So Saints from toil to praise & glory goe.

O gratefull Miriam in thy temper wrought
too warm for Silence or inventing thought
Thy part of anthem was to warble o're
In sweet response what Moses sung before.
Thou led the publick voice to Joyn his lays,
& words redoubling well redoubled praise.
Receive thy title, Prophetess was thine
When here thy Practice showd ye form divine.
The Spirit thus approvd, resignd in will
The Church bows down, & hears responses still.

Nor slightly suffer tunefull Jubals name
To miss his place among ye Sons of Fame,
Whose Sweet infusions coud of old inspire,
The breathing organs & ye trembling Lyre.
Father of these on earth, whose gentle Soul
By such ingagements coud ye mind controul,
If holy verses ought to Musick owe,
Be that thy large account of thanks below,
Whilst then ye timbrels lively pleasure gave,
& now whilst organs Sound Sedately grave.

My first attempt ye finishd course commends,
Now Fancy flagg not as that subject ends,
But charmd with beautys which attend thy way,
Ascend harmonious in the next essay.
So flys ye Lark, (& learn from her to fly)
She mounts, she warbles in ye wind on high,
She falls from thence, & seems to drop her wing,
But e're she lights to rest remounts to sing.

It is not farr the days have rolld their years,
Before the Second brightend work appears.
It is not farr, Alas the faulty cause

Which from the Prophet sad reflection draws!
Alas that blessings in possession cloy,
& peevish murmurs are preferrd to Joy,
That favourd Israel coud be faithless still,
& question Gods protecting power or will,
Or dread devoted Canaans warlike men,
& Long for Ægypt & their bonds again.

Scarce thrice the Sun since hardend Pharaoh dyd
As bridegrooms issue forth with glitt'ring pride
Rejoycing rose, & lett ye nation See
three Shining days of easy liberty,
Ere the mean fears of want producd within
Vain thought replenishd with rebellious Sin.
O Look not Israel to thy former way,
God cannot fail, & either wait or pray.
Within the borders of thy promisd Lands,
Lots hapless wife a strange example stands,
She turnd her eyes & felt her change begin,
& wrath as fierce may meet resembling Sin.
Then forward move thy camp & forward Still,
& lett sweet mercy bend thy Stubborn will.

At thy complaint a branch in Marah cast
With sweetning virtue mends ye waters tast.
At thy complaint the Lab'ring Tempest sailes,
& drives afore a wondrous showr of Quailes.
On tender grass the falling Manna lyes,
& Heav'n it self the want of bread supplys.
The rock divided flows upon the plain,
At thy complaint, & still thou wil't complain.
As thus employd thou went ye desart through,
Lo Sinai mount upreard its head to view.
Thine eyes perceivd the darkly-rolling cloud,
Thine ears the trumpet shrill ye thunder loud,
The forky lightning shot in livid gleam,
The Smoke arose, ye mountain all aflame
Quak'd to ye depths, & worked with signs of awe,
While God descended to dispense the law.
Yet neither mercy manifest in might
Nor pow'r in terrour coud preserve thee right.

Provokt with crimes of such an heinous kind
Allmighty Justice sware the doom designd,
That these shoud never reach ye promisd seat,
& Moses gently mourns their hastend fate.

Ile think him now resignd to publick care,
While night on pitchy plumes slides soft in air.
Ile think him giving what ye guilty sleep
To thoughts where Sorrow glides & numbers weep,

Sad thoughts of woes that reign where Sins prevail,
& mans short life, tho' not so short as frail.
Within this circle for his inward eyes
He bids the fading low creation rise,
& streight a train of mimick Senses brings
The dusky shapes of transitory things,
Thro' pensive shades the visions seem to range,
They seem to flourish, & they seem to change;
A moon decreasing runs the silent sky,
The sickly birds on molting feathers fly,
Men walking count their days of blessings o're,
The blessings vanish & the tales no more,
Still hours of nightly watches steal away,
Big waters roll green blades of grass decay,
Then all ye Pensive shades by Just degrees
Grows faint confuses & goes off with these.
But while the affecting notions pass along,
He chuses such as best adorn his song,
& thus with God the rising lays began,
God ever reigning God, compard with man:
& thus they movd to man beneath his rod;
Man deeply sinning, man chastisd by God.

O Lord O Saviour, tho' thy chosen band
Have staid like strangers in a forreign land,
Through numberd ages which have run their race,
Still has thy mercy been our dwelling place.
Before the most exalted dust of earth,
The stately mountains had receivd a birth;
Before the pillars of the world were laid,
Before its habitable parts were made,
Thou wer't the God, from thee their rise they drew,
Thou great for ages great for ever too.

Man (mortall creature framd to feel decays)
Thine unresisted pow'r at pleasure sways,
Thou sayst return & parting Soules obey,
Thou sayst return & bodys fall to clay.
For whats a thousand fleeting years wth thee?
Or Time compard with long eternity,
Whose wings expanding infinitely vast,
Orestretch its utmost ends of first & last?
Tis like those hours that lately saw ye Sun,
He rose, & set, & all the day was don.
Or like the watches which dead night divide,
& while we slumber unregarded glide,
Where all ye present seems a thing of nought,
& past & future close to waking thought.

As raging floods, when rivers swell with rain,
Bear down ye groves & overflow ye plain,

So swift & strong thy wondrous might appears,
So Life is carryd down the rolling years.
As heavy sleep pursues the days retreat,
With dark with silent & unactive state,
So lifes attended on by certain doom,
& deaths ye rest, ye resting place a tomb.
It quickly rises & it guickly goes,
& youth its morning, age its evening shows.
Thus tender blades of grass, when beams diffuse,
Rise from the pressure of their early dews,
Point tow'rds ye skys their elevated spires,
& proudly flourish in their green attires,
But soon (ah fading state of things below!)
The Scyth destructive mows ye lovely show,
The rising Sun that Saw their glorys high
That Sun descending sees their glorys dy.

We still with more than common hast of fate
Are doomd to perish in thy kindled hate.
Our publick sins for publick Justice call,
& stand like markes on which thy Judgements fall.
Our secret sins that folly thought conceald
Are in thy light for punishment reveald.
Beneath the terrours of thy wrath divine
Our days unmixd with happiness decline,
Like empty storys tedious, short, & vain,
& never never more recalld again.

Yet what were Life, if to ye longest date
Which men have namd a life we backned fate?
Alas its most computed length appears
To reach ye limits but of Seav'nty years,
& if by strength to fourscore years we goe,
That strength is labour, & that labour woe.
Then will thy term expire, & thou must fly
O man O Creature surely born to dy.

But who regards a truth so throughly known?
Who dreads a wrath so manifestly shown?
Who seems to fear it tho' ye danger vyes
With any pitch to which our fear can rise?
O teach us so to number all our days
That these reflections may correct our ways,
That these may lead us from delusive dreams
To walk in heavnly wisdomes golden beams.

Return O Lord, how Long shall Israels sin
How Long thine anger be preservd within!
Before our times irrevocably past
Be kind be gracious & return at last.
Let Favour soon-dispensd our soules employ,

& long endure to make enduring Joy.
Send years of comforts for our years of woes,
Send these at least of equall length with those.
Shine on thy flock & on their offspring shine
With tender mercy (sweetest act divine).
Bright rays of Majesty serenely shed,
To rest in Glorys on the nations head.
Our future deeds with approbation bless,
& in the giving them give us success.

Thus with forgiveness earnestly desird,
Thus in the raptures of a bliss requird,
The man of God concludes his Sacred Strain,
Now sitt & see ye subject once again.

See Ghastly Death where Desarts all around
Spread forth their barren undelightfull ground:
There stalks the silent melancholly shade,
His naked bones reclining on a spade,
& thrice the spade with solemn sadness heaves,
& thrice earth opens in the form of graves,
His gates of darkness gape to take him in,
Then where he soon woud Sink he's pushed by sin.

Poor Mortalls here your common picture know,
& with your Selves in this acquainted grow.
Through life with airy thoughtless pride you range
& vainly glitter in the Sphear of change,
A sphear where all things but for time remain,
Where no fixd starrs with endless glory reign,
But Meteors onely short-lived Meteors rise
To shine shoot down & dy beneath ye skys.

There is an hour, Ah who yt hour attends!
When man ye guilded vanity descends.
When forreign force or wast of inward heat
Constrain ye soul to leave its ancient seat;
When banishd Beauty from her empire flyes,
& with a languish leaves ye Sparkling eyes;
When softning Musick & Persuasion fail,
& all the charms that in ye tongue prevail,
When Spirits stop their course, when nerves unbrace,
& outward action & perception cease.
'Tis then the poor deformd remains shall be
That naked Skeleton we seem to see.

Make this thy mirrour if thou woudst have bliss,
No flattring image shows it self in this;
But such as lays the lofty lookes of pride,
& makes cool thought in humble channel glide;
But such as clears ye cheats of Errours den,

Whence magick mists surround ye soules of men,
Whence Self-Delusions trains adorn their flight,
As Snows fair feathers fleet to darken sight,
Then rest, & in the work of Fancy spread
To gay-wavd plumes for ev'ry mortals head.
These empty Forms when Death appears disperse,
Or melt in tears upon its mournfull hearse,
The sad reflection forces men to know,
'Life surely failes & swiftly flys below.

O Least thy folly loose ye proffit sought
O never touch it with a glancing thought,
As men to glasses come, & straight wth draw,
& straight forgett what sort of face they saw:
But fix intently fix thine inward eyes,
& in the strength of this great truth be wise.
'If on ye globes dim Side our sences Stray,
'Not usd to perfect light we think it day:
'Death seems long sleep, & hopes of heavnly beams
'Deceitfull wishes big with distant dreams.
'But if our reason purge ye carnal sight,
'& place its objects in their Juster light,
'We change ye side, from Dreams on earth we move,
'& wake through death to rise in life above.

Here ore my soul a solemn silence reigns,
Preparing thought for new celestial strains.
The former vanish off, ye new begin,
The solemn silence stands like night between,
In whose dark bosome day departing lyes,
& day succeeding takes a lovely rise.
But tho' ye song be changd, be still ye flame,
& Still ye prophet in my lines ye Same,
With care renewd upon the children dwell,
Whose sinfull Fathers in the desart fell,
With care renewd (if any care can do)
Ah least they sin & least they perish too.

Go seek for Moses at yon Sacred tent
On which ye Presence makes a bright descent.
Behold ye cloud with radiant glory fair
Like a wreathd pillar curl its gold in air.
Behold it hovering Just above the door,
& Moses meekely kneeling on the floor.
But if the gazing turn thine edge of sight,
& darkness Spring from unsupported light,
Then change ye Sense, be sight in hearing drownd,
While these strange accents from the vision sound.
The time my Servant is approaching nigh
When thou shall't gatherd with thy Fathers ly,
& soon thy nation quite forgetfull grown

Of all the glorys which mine arm has shown,
Shall through my covenant perversely break,
Despise my worship & my name forsake,
By customes conquerd where to rule they go,
& Serving Gods that cant protect ye foe.
Displeasd at this Ile turn my face aside
Till sharp Afflictions rod reduce their pride
Till brought to better mind they seek relief,
By good confessions in the midst of grief.
Then write thy song to stand a witness still
Of favours past & of my future will,
For I their vain conceits before discern,
Then write thy Song which Israels sons shall learn.

As thus ye wondrous voice its charge repeats
The Prophet musing deep within retreats.
He Seems to feel it on a streaming ray
Pierce through ye Soul enlightning all its way.
& much Obedient will & free desire,
& much his Love of Jacobs Seed inspire,
& much O much above ye warmth of those
The Sacred Spirit in his bosome glows,
Majestick Notion Seems Decrees to nod,
& Holy Transport speakes ye words of God.

Returnd at length, the finishd roll he brings,
Enrichd with Strains of past & future things.
The Priests in order to ye tent repair,
The Gatherd Tribes attend their Elders there:
O Sacred Mercys inexhausted Store!
Shall these have warning of their faults before,
Shall these be told ye recompenses due,
Shall Heavn & Earth be calld to witness too!
Then still ye tumult if it will be so,
Its Fear to loose a word lett caution Show,
Lett close Attention in dead calm appear,
& softly softly steal with silence near,
While Moses raisd above ye listning throng,
Pronounces thus in all their ears the Song.

Hear O ye Heav'ns Creations lofty show,
Hear O thou heavn-encompassd Earth below.
As Silver Showrs of gently-dropping rain,
As Honyd Dews distilling on ye plain,
As rain as Dews for tender grass designd,
So shall my speeches sink within ye mind,
So sweetly turn ye Soules enlivening food,
So fill & cherish hopefull seeds of good.
For now my Numbers to the world Abroad,
Will lowdly celebrate ye name of God.

Ascribe thou nation, evry favourd tribe
Excelling greatness to ye Lord ascribe,
The Lord, the Rock on whom we safely trust,
Whose work is perfect, & whose ways are Just,
The Lord whose promise stands for ever true,
The Lord most righteous & most holy too.

Ah worse Election! Ah the bonds of sin!
They chuse themselves to take corruption in.
They stain their soules with vices deepest blots,
When onely frailtys are his childrens spots.
Their thoughts words actions all are run astray,
& none more crooked more perverse than they.

Say rebell Nation O unwisely light,
Say will thy folly thus thy God requite?
Or is He not the God who made thee free,
Whose mercy purchasd & establishd thee?

Remember well ye wondrous days of old,
The years of ages long before thee told,
Ask all thy fathers who the truth will show,
Or ask thine elders for thine elders know.

When ye most high with scepter pointed down
Describd ye Realms of each beginning Crown,
When Adams offspring Providentiall care
To people countrys scatterd here & there,
He so ye limits of their lands confind,
That favourd Israel has its part assignd,
For Israel is ye Lords, & gaines ye place
Reservd for those whom he woud chuse to grace.

Him in ye desart him his mercy found
Where famine dwells & howling deafs ye ground,
Where dread is felt by savage noise encreast,
Where solitude erects its seat on wast.
& there he led him, & he taught him there,
& safely kept him with a watchfull care,
The tender apples of our heedfull eye
Not more in guard nor more securely ly.
& as an eagle that attempts to bring
Her unexperiencd young to trust the wing,
Stirrs up her nest, & flutters ore their heads,
& all ye forces of her pinnions spreads,
& takes & bears ym on her plumes above,
To give peculiar proof of royall love,
Twas so ye Lord, the gracious Lord alone,
With kindness most peculiar led his own,
As no strange God concurrd to make him free,
So none had powr to lead him through but he.

To lands excelling lands & planted high
That boast ye kindlyest-influencing sky
He brought, he bore him on ye wings of Grace,
To tast ye plentys of ye grounds encrease,
Sweet-dropping hony from the rocky soil,
from flinty rocks ye smoothly-flowing oyl,
The guilded butter from the stately kine,
The milk with which ye duggs of sheep decline,
The marrow-fatness of the tender lambs,
The bulky breed of Basans goats & rams,
The finest flowry wheat that crowns the plain
Distends its husk & loads the blade with grain,
& still he drank from ripe delicious heaps
Of clusters pressd the purest blood of grapes.

But thou art waxen fatt & kickest now,
O Well-Directed O Jesurun thou.
Thou soon w'ert fatt, thy sides were thickly grown,
Thy fattness deeply coverd evry bone
Then wanton fullness vain oblivion brought,
& God that made & savd thee was forgott,
While Gods of forreign lands & rites abhorrd,
To Jealousys & anger movd ye Lord;
While Gods thy fathers never knew were ownd;
& Hell ev'n Hell with sacrifice attond.
Oh fooles unmindfull whence your orderd frame
& whence your life-infusing spirit came!
Such strange corruptions his revenge provoke,
& thus their fate his indignation spoke.

It is decreed. Ile hide my face & see
When I forsake them what their end shall be.
For they're a froward very froward strain,
That promisd duty but returnd disdain.
In my grievd soul they raise a Jealous flame
By new-namd Gods & onely Gods in name,
They make the burnings of mine anger glow
By guilty vanitys displeasing show:
Ile also teach their Jealousy to frett
At people not formd a people yet,
Ile make their anger vex their inward breast
When such as have not known my laws are blesst.
A fire a fire that nothing can asswage
Is kindled in the fierceness of my rage,
To burn the deeps, consume ye lands increase,
& on the mountains strong foundations seize.
Thick heaps of mischief on their heads I send,
& all mine arrows wingd with fury spend.
Slow-parching dearth & pestilentiall heat,
Shall bring the bitter pangs of lingring fate.
Sharp teeth of beasts shall swift destruction bring,

Dire serpents wound them with invenomd sting,
The sword without & dread within consume
The youth the virgin in their lovely bloom,
Weak tender Infancy by suckling fed,
& helpless age with hoary-frosted head.
I said Ide scatter all the sinfull race,
I said Ide make its meer remembrance cease,
But much I feard the foes unruly pride,
Their glory vaunted & my powr denyd,
While thus they boast, our arm has shown us brave,
& God did nothing, for he could not Save.
So fond their thought, so farr remote of sense,
& blind in every course of Providence.
O knew they rightly where my Judgements tend,
O woud they ponder on their latter end!
Soon woud they find, that when upon ye field
One makes a thousand two ten thousand yield,
The Lord of Hosts has Sold a rebel state,
The Lord inclosd it in ye netts of fate.
For whats anothers rock compard with ours,
Lett them be Judges that have provd their powrs,
That on their own have vainly calld for aid,
While ours to freedome & to glory led.
Their vine may seem indeed to flourish fair,
But yet it grows in Sodoms tainted air,
It sucks corruption from Gomorrahs fields,
Rank Galls for grapes in bitter clusters yields,
& poison sheds for wine, like yt which comes
from asps & Dragons death-infected gums;
& are not these their hatefull sins reveald,
& in my treasures for my Justice seald?
To me the province of revenge belongs,
To me the certain recompense of wrongs,
Their feet shall totter in appointed time,
& threatning danger overtake their crime,
For wingd with featherd hast ye minutes fly,
To bring those things that must afflict them nigh.
The Lord will Judge his own & bring ym low,
& then repent & turn upon ye foe,
& when the Judgements from his own remove,
Will thus the foe convincingly reprove.
Where are ye Gods ye rock to whom in vain
Your offrings have been made your victims slain?
Lett them arise, lett them afford their aid,
& with Protections shield surround your head.
Know then your maker, I the Lord am he,
Nor ever was there any God with me,
& death or life & wounds or health I give,
Nor can another from my powr reprieve.
With Solemn state I lift mine arm on high
Ore ye rich glorys of the lofty sky,

& by my self majestically swear,
I live for ever & for ever there.
If in my rage ye glitt'ring sword I whet,
& sternly sitting take ye Judgement seat,
My Just-awarding sentence dooms my foe,
& vengeance wields ye blade & gives ye blow,
& Deep in flesh ye blade of Fury bites,
& deadly-deep my bearded arrow lightes,
& both grow drunk with blood defild in sin,
When executions of revenge begin.

Then lett his nation in a common voice,
& with his nation lett ye world rejoyce.
For whether God for crimes or tryalls spill
His Servants blood, he will avenge it still.
He'le break ye troops, he'le scatter all afarr
Who vex our realm with desolating warr.
& on ye favour'd tribes & on their land
Shed Victorys & peace from Mercys hand.

Here ceasd ye song, & Israel lookd behind
& gazd before with unconfining mind,
& fixd in silence & amazement saw
The strokes of all their state beneath ye law.
Their Recollection does its light present
To show ye mountain blessd with Gods descent,
To show their wandrings, their unfixd abode,
& all their guidance in the desert road.
Then where the beams of Recollection goe
To leave ye fancy dispossessd of show,
The fairer light of Prophecy's begun
Which opening future days supplys their sun.
By such a sun (& fancy needs no more)
They see the coming times & walk ym o're,
& now they gain that rest their travel sought,
Now milk & hony stream along the thought,
Anon they fill their soules, ye blessings cloy,
& God's forgot in full excess of Joy.
& oft they sin, & oft his anger burns
& ev'ry nations made their scourge by turns,
Till oft repenting they convert to God,
& he repenting too destroys the rod.

O nation timely warnd in sacred strain,
O never lett thy Moses sing in vain.
Dare to be good & happiness prolong
Or if thy folly will fullfill the song,
At least be found the seldomer in ill,
& still repent & soon repent thee still.
When such fair paths thou shalt avoid to tread,
Thy blood will rest upon thy sinfull head,

Thy crime by lasting long secure thy foe,
The gracious warning to the Gentiles goe,
& all the world thats calld to witness here
convincd by thine example learn to fear.
The gentil world a mystick Israel grown
Will in thy first condition find their own,
A Gods descent, a Pilgrimage below,
& Promisd rest where living waters flow.
They'le see the pen describe in ev'ry trace,
The frowns of Anger, or the Smiles of Grace,
Why mercy turns aside & leaves to shine,
What cause provokes the Jealousy divine,
Why Justice kindles dire-avenging flames,
What endless powr ye Lifted Arm proclaims,
Why Mercy shines again with chearfull ray,
& Glory double-gilds ye lightsome day.
Tho Nations change & Israels empire dyes,
Yet still ye case which rose before may rise,
Eternall Providence its rule retains,
& still preserves, & still applys ye strains.

Twas such a gift ye Prophets sacred pen
On his departure left ye sons of men.
Thus he, & thus ye Swan her breath resigns
(Within ye beautys of Poetick lines,)
He white with innocence, his figure she,
& both harmonious, but the sweeter he.
Death learns to charm, & while it leads to bliss
Has found a lovely circumstance in this
To suit the meekest turn of easy mind,
& actions chearfull in an air resignd.

Thou flock whom Moses to thy freedome led
How will't thou lay the venerable dead?
Go (if thy Fathers taught a work they knew)
Go build a Pyramid to Glory due,
Square ye broad base, with sloping sides arise,
& lett the point diminish in the skys.
There leave the corps, suspending ore his head
The wand whose motion winds & waves obeyd.
On Sabled Banners to ye sight describe
The painted arms of evry mourning tribe,
& thus may publick grief adorn ye tomb
Deep-streaming downwards through ye vaulted room.
On the black stone a fair inscription raise
That Sums his Government to speak his praise,
& may the style as brightly worth proclaim,
As if Affection with a pointed beam
Engravd or fird ye words, or Honour due
Had with its self inlaid ye tablet through.

But stop ye pomp that is not mans to pay,
For God will grace him in a nobler way.
Mine eyes perceive an orb of heavnly state
With splendid forms & light serene repleat,
I hear the Sound of fluttring wings in air,
I hear the tunefull tongues of Angels there,
They fly, they bear, they rest on Nebo's head,
& in thick glory wrap the rev'rend dead.
This errand crowns his songs, & tends to prove
His near communion with ye quire above.
Now swiftly down the Steepy mount they go,
Now swiftly glides their shining orb below,
& now moves off where rising grounds deny
To spread their vally to the distant eye.
Ye blessd inhabitants of glitt'ring air
You've born ye prophet but we know not where.
Perhaps least Israel overfondly led
In rating worth when envy leaves ye dead,
Might plant a grove, invent new rites divine,
Make him their Idol, & his grave ye shrine.

But what disorder? what repells ye light
& ere its season forces up ye night?
Why sweep the spectres ore ye blasted ground?
What shakes ye mount with hollow-roaring sound?
Hell rolls beneath it, Terrour stalkes before
With shriekes & groans, & Horrour bursts a door,
& Satan rises in infernall state
Drawn up by Malice Envy Rage & Hate.
A darkning Vapour with sulphureous steam,
In pitchy curlings, edgd by sullen flame,
& framd a chariot for ye dreadfull Form,
Drives whirling up on mad Confusions storm.

Then fiercely turning where ye Prophet dyd,
Nor shall thy nation scape my wrath he cry'd;
This corps Ile enter & thy flock mislead,
& all thy Miracles my lyes shall aid.
But where?—Hes gon, & by ye scented sky
The fav'rite courtiers have been lately nigh.
O slow to buisness, cursd in mischiefs hour,
Track on their Odours, & if Hell has powr—
This said with spight & with a bent for ill
He shot in fury from ye trembling hill.

In vain Proud Fiend thy threats are half exprest,
& half ly choaking in thy scornfull breast,
His shining bearers have performd ye rite,
& laid him softly down in shades of night.
A Warriour heads ye band, Great Michael he,
Renownd for conquest in ye warr with thee,

A sword of flame to stop thy course he bears,
Nor has thy rage availd, nor can thy snares,
The Lord rebuke thy pride he meekly cryes:
The Lord has heard him & thy project dyes.

Here Moses leaves my song, ye tribes retire,
The desert flyes, & fourty years expire.
& now my fancy for awhile be still,
& think of coming down from Nebo's hill.
Go Search among thy forms, & thence prepare
A cloud in folds of Soft-surrounding air,
Go find a breeze to lift thy cloud on high,
To waft thee gently rockd in open sky,
Then stealing back to leave a silent calm,
& thee reposing in a grove of palm.
The place will suit my next-succeeding strain,
& Ile awake thee soon to sing again.

Hannah

Now Crowds more off, retiring trumpetts sound
On Eccho's dying in their last rebound,
The notes of fancy seem no longer strong,
But sweetning closes fitt a private song.
So when the storms forsake ye seas command
To break their forces in the winding land,
No more their blasts tumultuous rage proclaim,
But sweep in murmurs ore a murm'ring stream.

Then Seek ye Subject & its song be mine
Whose numbers next in Sacred story shine;
Go brightly-working thought, prepard to fly
Above ye page on hov'ring pinnions ly,
& beat with stronger force to make thee rise
Where beautious Hannah meets ye searching eyes.

There frame a town & fix a tent with cords,
The town be Shiloh calld, the tent ye Lords.
Carvd pillars filleted with silver rear
To close ye curtains in an outward square,
But those within it which ye porch uphold
Be finely wrought & overlaid with gold.

Here Eli comes to take ye resting Seat,
Slow-moving forward with a revrend gate,
Sacred in office, venerably sage
& venerably great in silverd age.

Here Hannah comes, a melancholly wife

Reproachd for barren in ye marriage life.
Like summer-mornings she to sight appears,
Bedewd & shining in the midst of tears.
Her heart in bitterness of grief she bowd,
& thus her wishes to the Lord she vowd.
If thou thine handmaid with compassion see,
If I my God am not forgott by thee,
If in mine offspring thou prolong my line,
The Child I wish for all his days be thine,
His life devoted in thy courts be led,
& not a rasour come upon his head.

So from recesses of her inmost soul
Through moving lips her still devotion stole:
As silent waters glide through parted trees
Whose branches tremble with a rising breeze.
The words were lost because her heart was low,
But free desire had taught ye mouth to go.
This Eli markd, & with a voice severe,
While yet she multiplyd her thoughts in prayr,
How long shall wine he crys distract thy breast,
Begon & lay ye drunken fitt by rest.
Ah says ye mourner count not this for sin,
It is not wine but grief that workes within,
The spirit of thy wretched handmaid know,
Her prayr's complaint, & her condition woe.
Then spake ye Sacred Priest, in peace depart,
& with thy comfort God fullfill thine heart.
His blessing thus pronouncd with awfull sound,
The Vot'ry bending leaves ye solemn ground,
She seems confirmd the Lord has heard her crys,
& Chearfull Hope the tears of trouble drys,
& makes her alterd eyes irradiate roll
With Joy that dawns in thought upon ye soul.

Now lett ye Town & Tent & court remain,
& leap the time till Hannah comes again.
As painted prospects skip along ye green
from hills to mountains eminently seen,
& leave their intervalls that sink below
In deep retirement unexpressd to show.

Behold she comes (but not as once she came
To grieve to sigh & teach her eyes to stream.)
Content adorns her with a lively face,
An open look, & smiling kind of grace.
Her little Samuel in her arms she bears
The wish of long desire & Child of prayrs,
& as ye sacrifice she brought begun,
To rev'rend Eli she presents her son.
Here, crys ye Mother, here my Lord may see

The woman come who prayd in grief by thee,
The Child I su'd for God with bounty gave,
& what he granted let him now receive.

But still ye Vot'ry feeles her temper move
With all ye tender violence of Love.
That still enjoys ye gift, & inly burns
To search for larger or for more returns.
Then filld with blessings which allure to praise,
& raisd by Joy to soul-enchanting lays,
Thus thankes ye Lord beneficently-kind
In sweet effusions of ye gratefull mind.

My lifting heart with more than common heat
Sends up its thankes to God on ev'ry beat.
My glory raisd above ye reach of scorn
In God exalts its highly-planted horn.
My mouth enlargd mine enemy defys,
& finds in Gods salvation full replys.
O Bright in holy beautys, Powr divine,
Theres none whose glory can compare wth thine,
None share thine honours, nay theres none beside,
No rock on which thy creatures can confide.

Ye proud in spirit who your gifts adore,
Unlearn the fault & speak with pride no more:
No more in words your arrogance be shown,
Nor call ye workes of Providence your own,
Since he that rules us infinitely knows,
& as he will his acts of Powr dispose.

The strong whose sinewy forces archd ye bow
Have seen it shatterd by ye conqu'ring foe.
The weak have felt their nerves more firmly brace,
& new-sprung vigour in the limbs encrease.
The full whom varyd tasts of plenty fed
Have lett their labour out to gain their bread.
The poor that languishd in a starving state
Content & full have ceased to beg their meat.
The barren womb, no longer barren now,
(O be my thankes accepted with my vow)
In pleasure wonders at a mothers pain,
& sees her offspring & conceives again,
While she that gloryd in her numerous heirs,
Now broke by feebleness no longer bears.

Such turns their rising from ye Lord derive,
The Lord that kills the Lord yt makes alive.
He brings by sickness down to gaping graves,
& by restoring health from sickness saves;

He makes ye poor by keeping back his store,
& makes ye rich by blessing men with more;
He sinking hearts with bitter grief annoys,
Or lifts them bounding with enlivend Joys.

He takes ye beggar from his humble clay
From off ye dunghill where despisd he lay
To mix with Princes in a rank supream,
Fill thrones of Honour & inherit fame.
For all the pillars of exalted state
So nobly firm so beautifully great,
Whose various orders bear ye rounded ball
Which woud without them to confusion fall,
All are ye Lords, at his disposure stand,
& prop ye governd world at his command.

His mercy still more wonderfully sweet
Shall guard ye righteous & uphold their feet.
While through ye darkness of ye wicked soul
Amazement Dread & Desperation roll,
While envy stops their tongues, & hopeless grief
That sees their fears but not their fears relief,
& they their strength as unavailing view,
Since none shall trust in that & safely too.

The foes of Israel for his Israels sake
God will to pieces in his anger break.
His bolts of thunder from an opend sky
Shall on their heads with force unerring fly.
His voice shall call, & all ye world shall hear,
& all for sentence at his Seat appear.

But mount to gentler praises, mount again
My thought prophetick of Messiahs reign,
Perceive the glorys which around him shine,
& thus thine hymn be crownd with grace divine.
'Strength to ye King for mans salvation born,
'& honours rising like ye lifted horn.

Tis here ye numbers find a bright repose,
The vows accepted & the Vot'ry goes.
But thou my soul upon her accents hung,
& sweetly pleasd with what she sweetly sung,
Prolong the pleasure with thine inward eyes,
Turn back thy thought, & see ye subject rise.

In her peculiar case ye song begun,
& for awhile through private blessings run,
As through their banks the curling waters play,
& soft in murmurs kiss ye flowry way.
With force encreasing then she leaps ye bounds,

& largely flows on more extended grounds,
Spreads wide & wider, till vast seas appear,
& boundless views of Providence are here.

How Swift these views along her Anthem glide,
As waves on waves pushd forward in ye tide!
How swift thy wonders ore my fancy sweep,
O Providence thou great unfathomd deep,
Where Resignation gently dips ye wing,
& learns to love & thank, admire & sing,
But bold presumptious Reasnings diving down
To reach ye bottom, in their diving drown.

Neglecting man forgetfull of thy ways
Nor owns thy care, nor thinkes of giving praise,
But from himself his happiness derives,
& thankes his wisdome when by thine he thrives.
His limbs at ease in soft repose he spreads,
Bewitchd with vain delights on flowry beds,
& while his sense ye fragrant breezes kiss,
He meditates a waking dream of bliss.
He thinks of Kingdomes & their crowns are near;
He thinkes of glorys & their rays appear;
He thinks of beautys & a lovely face
Serenely smiles in evry taking grace;
He thinks of riches & their heaps arise
Display their glittring forms & fix his eyes;
Thus drawn with pleasures in a charming view
Rising he reaches & woud faign pursue.
But still ye fleeting shadows mock his care,
& still his fingers grasp at yielding air,
What ere our tempers as their comforts want
It is not mans to take but Gods to grant.

If then persisting in the vain design
We seek true bliss unblessd with help divine,
Still may we search, still search without relief,
Nor onely want a bliss but find a grief.
That such conviction may to sight appear
Sitt down ye Sons of men spectatours here,
Behold a scene upon your folly wrought,
& lett this lively scene instruct ye thought.

Boy blow thy pipe untill ye bubble rise,
Then cast it off to float upon ye skys,
Still swell its sides with breath. O beautious frame!
It grows, it shines, be now the world thy name.
Methinks Creation forms itself within,
The men, the towns, ye birds, ye trees are seen,
The skys above present an Azure show,
& lovely Verdure paints an earth below.

Ile wind my self in this delightfull sphere,
& live a thousand years of pleasure there,
Rolld up in blisses which around me close,
& now regald with these & now with those.
False hope, but falser words of Joy farewell,
You've rent the lodging where I meant to dwell,
My bubble's burst, my prospects disappear,
& leave behind a moral & a tear.

If at the type our dreaming soules awake,
& Hannahs strains their Just impression make,
The boundless powr of Providence we know,
& fix our trust on nothing here below.
Then He grown pleasd that men his greatness own,
Lookes down Serenely from his starry throne,
& bids ye blessed days our prayrs have won
Put on their glorys & prepare to run.
For which our thanks be Justly sent above,
Enlargd by gladness, & inspird with Love:
For which his praises be for ever sung,
Oh Sweet employments of ye gratefull tongue!

Burst forth my temper in a godly flame,
For all his blessings laud his holy name:
That ere mine eyes saluted chearfull day
A gift devoted in ye womb I lay,
Like Samuel vowd before my breath I drew,
O coud I prove in life like Samuel too!
That all my frame is exquisitely wrought,
The world enjoyd by sense, & God by thought;
That living streams through living Channels glide
To make this frame by natures course abide;
That for its good by Providences care
Fire Joyns with water, earth concurrs wth air;
That Mercys ever-inexhausted store
Is pleasd to proffer & to promise more,
& all ye proffers stream with grace divine,
& all ye promises with glory shine.
O praise the Lord my Soul, in one accord
Lett all that is within me praise ye Lord;
O praise ye Lord my soul, & ever strive
To keep the sweet remembrances alive:
Still raise ye kind affections of thine heart,
Raise evry gratefull word to bear a part,
With ev'ry word the strains of love devise,
Awake thine harp, & thou thy self arise,
Then if his Mercy be not half expresst,
Lett wondring silence magnify ye rest.

Deborah

Time Sire of years unwind thy leaf anew,
& still the past recall to present view,
Spread forth its circles, swiftly gaze ym ore,
But where an action's nobly sung before
There stop & stay for me whose thoughts design
To make anothers song resound in mine.
Pass where ye priests procession bore the law,
When Jourdans parted waters fixd with awe,
While Israel marchd upon ye naked Sand,
Admird ye wonder, & obtaind the land.
Slide through the num'rous fates of Canaans kings,
While conquest rode on Expeditions wings.
Glance over Israel at a single view
In bondage oft, & oft unbound anew,
Till Jabin rise, & Deborah stand enrolld
On the broad guilded leafs revolving fold.

O King subdu'd! O Woman born to fame!
O Wake my fancy for the glorious theme,
O wake my fancy with the sense of praise,
O wake with warblings of triumphant lays.
The Land you rise in sultry suns invade,
But where you rise to sing you'le find a shade.

Those trees in order & with verdure crownd,
The Sacred Prophetesses tent surround.
& that fair palm afront exactly plact
That overtops & overspreads the rest,
Near ye broad root a mossy bank supports,
Where Justice opens unexpensive courts.
There Deb'rah sits, the willing tribes repair,
Referr their causes, & she Judges there.
Nor needs a guard to bring her subjects in,
Each Grace each Virtue proves a guard unseen.
Nor wants the penaltys enforcing law,
While Great Opinion gives effectuall awe.

Now twenty years that rolld in heavy pain
Saw Jabin gall them with Oppressions chain,
When she submissive to divine command,
Proclaims a warr for freedome o're ye land,
& bids young Barack with those men descend,
Whom in the mountains he for battle traind.
Go, says the Prophetess, thy foes assail,
Go make ten thousand over all prevail,
Make Jabins captains feel thy glittering sword,
Make all his army: God has spoke the word.
He fitt for warr & Israels hope in sight
Yet doubts ye number & by that the fight,

Then thus replys with wish to stand secure,
Or eager thought to know the conquest sure:
Belovd of God, lend thou thy presence too
& I with gladness lead th' appointed few,
But if thou wil't not lett thy son deny,
For whats ten thousand men or what am I?
If so, she crys, a share of toil be mine,
Another share & some dishonour thine,
For God to punish doubt resolves to show
That less than numbers can suppress his foe;
You'le move to conquer, & the foes to yield,
But 'tis a womans act assures the field.

Now seem the warriours in their ranks assignd,
Now furling banners flutter in the wind,
Her words encourage, & his actions lead,
Hope spurrs them forward, valour draws ye blade,
& Freedome like a fair reward for all
Stands reaching forth her hand & seems to call.

On T'other side & allmost ore ye plain
Proud Sis'ra Jabins captain brings his men,
As thick as locusts on the vintage fly,
As thick as scatterd leaves in Autumn ly,
Bold with success against a nation tryd,
& proud of numbers, & secure in pride.

Now sound the trumpets, now my fancy warms,
& now methinks I view their toiles in arms,
The lively Phantomes tread my boundless mind
With no faint colours or weak strokes designd.
See where in distant conflict from afarr
The pointed arrows bring the wounds of warr.
See where the lines with closer force engage,
& thrust the spear & whirl ye sword of rage.
Here break the files & vainly strive to close,
There on their own repelld assist their foes.
Here Deb'rah calls & Jabins souldiers fly,
There Barack fights & Jabins souldiers dy.
But now nine hundred chariots roll along,
Expert their guiders & their horses strong,
& Terrour rattling in their fierce array
Bears down on Israel to restore the day.
O Lord of battles, O the dangers near,
Assist thine Israel or they perish here.
How swift is Mercys aid, behold it fly
On rushing tempests through ye troubled sky,
With dashing rain with pelting hail they blow,
& sharply drive them on the facing foe,
Thus blessd with help & onely touchd behind,
The fav'rite Nation presses in the wind.

But heat of action now disturbs ye sight,
& wild confusion mingles all ye fight,
Cold-whistling winds & shriekes of dying men
& groans & armour sound in all ye plain.
The bands of Canaan fate no longer dare,
Oppressd by weather & destroyd by warr,
& from his chariot whence he ruld ye fight,
Their haughty Leader leaps to Joyn ye flight.
See where he flys, & see the Victour near,
See rapid Conquest in pursuit of Fear,
See See they both make off, ye work is ore,
& fancy cleard of vision as before.

Thus (if ye mind of man may seem to move
With some resemblance of ye skyes above)
When warrs are gath'ring in our hearts below
We've seen their battles in Ætheriall show:
The Long-distended tracts of opening sky
The Phantoms Azure field of fight supply;
The whitish clouds an argent armour yield;
A radiant blazon guilds their argent shield;
Young glittring comets point ye leveld spear,
Which for the pennons hang their flaming hair;
& ore their helms for gallant glory dresst
Sit curles of air & nod upon the crest.
Thus armd they seem to march & seem to fight,
& seeming wounds & deaths delude ye sight,
The ruddy thunder-clouds look staind with gore,
& for ye din of warr within they roar.
Then flys a side, & then a side pursues,
Till in the motion all their shapes they loose,
Dispersing air concludes ye mimick scene,
The sky shuts up & swiftly clears again.

But does their Sis'ra share ye common fate,
Or mourn his humbled pride in dark retreat?
With such enquiry near the palm repair,
Victorious Honour knows & tells it there.

To that fair type of Israels late success
Which nobly rises as its weights depress,
To that fair type returns ye Joyfull band,
Whose courage rose to free their groaning land,
There stands ye Leader in the pomp of arms,
There stands the Judge in beautys awfull charms.
& whilst reclind upon the resting spear
He pants with chace & breaths in calmer air,
Her thoughts are working with a backward view,
& woud in song the great exploit renew.

She sees an armd Oppressions hundred hands

impose its fetters on the promisd lands.
She sees her nation struggling in the chains,
& warrs arising with unequall trains.
She sees their feats in arms, the field embru'd,
The foe disorderd, & the foe pursud.
Till Conquest dressd in rays of Glory come
With Peace & Freedome brought in triumph home.
Then round her heart a beamy gladness plays,
Which darting forward thus converts to praise.

For Israels late avengings on ye foe
When led by no compelling powr below,
When each sprung forward of their own accord,
For this, for all the mercy praise the Lord.

Hear O ye Kings, ye neighbring Princes hear,
My song triumphant shall instruct your fear,
My song triumphant bids your glory bow
To God confessd the God of Jacob now.

O Glorious Lord when with thy sov'raign hand
Thou led thy nation off from Edoms Land,
Then trembled Earth, & shook ye Heav'ns on high,
& clouds in drops forsook ye melted sky,
With tumbling waters hills were heard to roar,
& felt such shocks as Sinai felt before.

But fear abating which by time decays,
The Kings of Canaan rose in Shamgars days,
& still continud into Jaels times
Their empire fixing with succesfull crimes.
Oppression ravagd all our lost abodes,
Nor durst ye people trust ye common roads,
But paths perplexd & unfrequented chose
To shun the dangers of insulting foes.
Thus direfull wast deformd ye country round,
Unpeopled towns & disimprovd the ground.
Till I resolving in the gap to stand
I Deb'rah rose a Mother of the Land,
Where others slaves by settled custome grown
Coud serve & chuse to serve the Gods unknown,
Where others sufferd with a tame regrett
Destruction spilling blood in ev'ry gate,
& fourty thousand had not for the field
One spear offensive or defensive shield.

O towrds ye Leaders of my nation move
O beat my warming heart with sense of love,
Commend th' Assertours on their own accord,
& bless ye Sovreign causer, bless the Lord.

Speak ye that ride with powr returnd in state,
Speak ye the praise that rule ye Judgement seat,
Speak ye the praise to God that walk ye roads,
While Safety brings you to restord abodes.

The rescud villagers no more affraid
Of Archers lurking in the faithless Shade,
& sudden death conveyd from sounding strings,
Shall safe-approach ye waters rising springs,
& while their turns of drawing there they wait,
Loytring in ease upon a grassy Seat,
Call all ye blessing of ye Lord to mind,
& sing the Lord in all ye blessing kind.
The townsmen rescud from ye tyrants reign
Shall flock with Joy to fill their walls again,
See Justice in ye gates her ballance bear,
& none but her unsheath a weapon there.

Awake O Deb'rah, O Awake to praise,
Awake & utter forth triumphant lays,
Arise O Barack, be thy pomp begun,
Lead on thy triumph thou Abinoams Son,
Thy captives bound in chains when Gods Decree
Made humbled Princes stoop their necks to thee,
When He the Giver of Success in fight
Advancd a Woman Ore ye Sons of Might.

Against this Amalek of banded foes
I Deb'rah root of All ye warr arose,
From Ephraim sprung, & leading Ephraims line,
The next in rising Benjamin was thine.
The ruling heads of half Manassehs land
To serve in danger left their safe command.
The tribe of Zebuluns unactive men
For Glorious arms forsook ye peacefull pen.
The Lords of Issachar with Deb'rah went,
The tribe with Barack to ye vale was sent,
Where he on foot performd the gen'ralls part,
& shard ye souldiers toil to raise their heart.

But Reubens strange divisions Justly wrought
Amongst his brethren deep concern of thought.
Ah while ye nation in affliction lay,
How coudst thou Reuben by ye sheepfold stay?
& lett thy bleating flock divert ye days
That idely passd thee with inglorious ease.
Divided Tribe, without thy danger free,
Deep were the Searchings of our hearts for thee.
Our Gilead too by such example swayd
With unconcern beyond ye river staid,
& Dan in ships at sea for safety rode,

& frighted Asher in its rocks abode.

Now Sing ye field, ye feats of warr begun,
& Praise thy Nepthali with Zebulun.
To deaths exposd, in posts advancd they stood,
With soules resolvd & gallant rage of blood.
Then came ye Kings & fought, ye Gatherd Kings
By waters streaming from Megiddo's springs,
In Tanaach vale sustaind ye daring toil,
Yet neither fought for pay, nor won ye spoil.
The skys indulgent to the cause of right
On Israels side against their army fight;
In evil aspects starrs & Planets range,
& by the weather in tempestuous change
Promote their dire distress, & make it known
That God has hosts above to save his own.
The Kishon swelld, grew rapid as they fled,
& rolld them sinking down its sandy bed.
O River Kishon, River of renown!
& O my soul that trod their glory down!
The stony paths by which disorderd flight
Conveyd their troops & chariots from ye fight
With rugged points their horses hoofs distresst,
& broke them prancing in impetuous hast.

Curse curse ye Meroz, curse ye town abhorrd,
(So spake ye glorious Angel of ye Lord.)
For Meroz came not into field prepard
To Joyn that side on which the Lord declard.

But bless ye Jael, be ye Kenites name
Above our womens blessd in endless fame.
The Captain faint with sore fatigue of flight,
Implord for water to support his might,
& milk she powrd him while he water sought,
& in a lordly dish her butter brought.
With courage well deserving to prevail
One hand her hammer held & one ye nail,
& him reclind to sleep she boldly slew,
She Smote, she piercd, she struck ye temples through,
Before her feet reluctant on the clay
He bowd he fell, he bowd he fell he lay,
He bowd he fell he dyd. by such degrees
As thrice she struck each strokes effect she sees.

His mother gazd with long-expecting eyes,
& grown impatient through ye lattice cryes;
Why moves ye chariot of my son so slow?
Or what affairs retard his coming so?
Her Ladys answerd.—but she woud not stay,
(For Pride had taught what Flattry meant to say)

They've sped she says, & now ye prey they share,
For each a damsel or a lovely pair,
For Sis'ras part a robe of gallant grace
Where diverse colours rich embroid'ry trace,
Meet for ye necks of those who win ye spoil
When triumph offers its reward for toil.

Thus perish all who Gods decrees oppose,
Thus like ye vanquishd perish all thy foes.
But lett ye men that in thy name delight
Be like ye Sun in heavnly glory bright,
When mounted on ye dawn he posts away,
& with full strength encreases on the day.

Twas here ye Prophetess respird fm song.
Then loudly shouted all ye chearfull throng,
By freedome gaind, by victory compleat,
Prepard for mirth irregularly great.
The frowns of sorrow gave their ancient place
To pleasure drawn in smiles on ev'ry face.
The groans of slav'ry were no longer wrung,
But thoughts of comfort from ye blessing sprung.
& as they shouted in ye breezy west,
Amongst ye plumes that deckt ye singers crest
The Spirit of Applause it self conveyd
On waving air, & lightly wanton plaid.
Such was ye case, (or such Ideas flow
From thought replenishd with triumphant show.)

What raisd their Joy their love coud also raise,
& each contended in the words of praise,
& evry word proclaimd the wonders past,
& God was still ye first & still ye last,
Deep in their soules ye fair impression lay,
Deep-tracd & never to be worn away.

From hence ye rescud generation still
Abhorrd the practice of rebellious ill,
& feard the punishment for ill abhorrd,
& lovd repentance & adord ye Lord.

From hence in all their day ye Lord was kind,
His face serene with settled favour shind,
Fair banishd Order was recalld in state,
The Laws revivd, the princes ruld ye gate,
Peace cheard ye vales, Contentment laughd wth Peace,
Gay-blooming Plenty rose with large encrease,
Sweet Mercy those who thought on mercy blesst,
& so for fourty years ye land had rest.

Rest happy Land awhile, ah longer so

didst thou thine happiness sincerely know!
But soon thy quiet with thy goodness past,
& in the song alone obtaind to last.

Live song triumphant, live in fair record,
& teach succeeding times to love ye Lord:
For fancy moves by bright example wood,
& wins ye mind with images of good.

Touchd with a sacred rage & heavnly flame,
I strive to sing thine universall aim,
To quit ye subject, & in lays sublime
The morall fitt for any point of time:
Then go my verses with applying strain
Go form a triumph not ascribd to men.

Lett all ye clouds of Grief impending ly,
& storms of Trouble drive along ye sky,
Then Humble Piety thine accents raise,
For prayr will prove ye powrfull charm of ease.

Lo now thy soul has spoke its best desires,
How blessings answer what ye prayr requires.
Before thy sighs the cloudes of Grief retreat,
The Storms of trouble by thy tears abate,
& Radiant Glory from her upper sphear
Lookes down & glitters in relented air.

Rise Lovely Piety from earthy bed,
The Parted flame descends upon thine head,
This wondrous Mitre framd by Sacred Love,
& for thy triumph sent thee from above,
In two bright points with upper rays aspires,
& rounds thy temples with innocuous fires.
Rise Lovely Piety, with Pomp appear,
& thou Kind Mercy Lend a chariot here,
On either side fair Fame & Honour place,
Behind lett Plenty walk in hand with peace,
While Irreligion mutt'ring horrid sound
With fierce & proud Oppression backward bound
Dragg by the wheeles along ye dusty plain,
& gnashing lick ye ground, & curse with pain.

Now come ye thousands & more thousands yet,
With order Joyn to fill ye train of state,
Soules tund for praising to ye temple bring,
& thus amidst ye Sacred Musick sing.
Hail Piety! triumphant Goodness hail!
Hail O prevailing! Ever O prevail!
At thine Entreaty Justice leaves to frown,
& Wrath appeasing lays ye Thunder down,

The tender heart of yearning Mercy burns,
Love asks a blessing & ye Lord returns.
In his great name that heavn & earth has made
In his great name alone we find our aid,
Then bless the Name, & lett ye world adore
From this time forward & for evermore.

Moses

To grace those lines wch next appear to sight,
The Pencil shone with more abated light,
Yet still ye pencil shone, ye lines were fair,
& awfull Moses stands recorded there.
Lett his repleat with flames & praise divine
Lett his the first-rememberd Song be mine.
Then rise my thought, & in thy Prophet find
What Joy shoud warm thee for ye work designd.
To that great act which raisd his heart repair,
& find a portion of his Spirit there.

A Nation helpless & unarmd I view,
Whom strong revengefull troops of warr pursue,
Seas Stop their flight, their camp must prove their grave.
Ah what can Save them? God alone can save.
Gods wondrous voice proclaims his high command,
He bids their Leader wave the sacred wand,
& where the billows flowd they flow no more,
A road lyes naked & they march it o're.
Safe may the Sons of Jacob travell through,
But why will Hardend Ægypt venture too?
Vain in thy rage to think the waters flee,
& rise like walls on either hand for thee.
The night comes on the Season for surprize,
Yet fear not Israel God directs thine eyes,
A fiery cloud I see thine Angel ride,
His Chariot is thy light & he thy guide.
The day comes on & half thy succours fail,
Yet fear not Israel God will still prevail,
I see thine Angel from before thee go,
To make the wheeles of ventrous Ægypt slow,
His rolling cloud inwraps its beams of light,
& what supplyd thy day prolongs their night.
At length the dangers of the deep are run,
The Further brink is past, the bank is won,
The Leader turns to view the foes behind,
Then waves his solemn wand within the wind.
O Nation freed by wonders cease thy fear,
& stand & see the Lords salvation here.

Ye tempests now from ev'ry corner fly,
& wildly rage in all my fancyd Sky.
Roll on ye waters as ye rolld before,
Ye billows of my fancyd ocean roar,
Dash high, ride foaming, mingle all ye main.
Tis don—& Pharaoh cant afflict again.
The work the wondrous work of Freedomes don,
The winds abate, the clouds restore ye Sun,
The wreck appears, the threatning army drownd
Floats ore ye waves to strow the Sandy ground.

Then Place thy Moses near the calming flood,
Majestically mild, serenely good.
Lett Meekness (Lovely virtue) gently Stream
Around his visage like a lambent flame.
Lett gratefull Sentiments, lett Sense of love,
Lett holy zeal within his bosome move.
& while his People gaze ye watry plain,
& fears last touches like to doubt remain,
While bright astonishment that seems to raise
A questioning belief, is fond to praise,
Be thus the rapture in the Prophets breast,
Be thus the thankes for freedome gaind expresst.

Ile sing to God, Ile Sing ye songs of praise
To God triumphant in his wondrous ways,
To God whose glorys in the Seas excell,
Where the proud horse & prouder rider fell.

The Lord in mercy kind in Justice strong
Is now my strength, this Strength be now my song,
This sure salvation, (such he proves to me
from danger rescu'd & from bondage free).
The Lords my God & Ile prepare his seat,
My Fathers God & Ile proclaim him great,
Him Lord of Battles, him renownd in name,
Him ever faithfull, evermore the same.

His gracious aids avenge his peoples thrall,
They make the pride of boasting Pharaoh fall.
Within the Seas his stately Chariots ly,
Within the Seas his chosen Captains dy.
The rolling deeps have coverd o're the foe,
They sunk like stones they Swiftly sunk below.
There O my God thine hand confessd thy care,
Thine hand was glorious in thy power there,
It broke their troops unequall for the fight
In all the greatness of excelling might.
Thy wrath Sent forward on ye raging Stream,
Swift sure & Sudden their destruction came,
They fell as stubble burns, while driving skys

Provoke & whirl a flame & ruin fly's.

When blasts dispatchd with wonderfull intent
On soveraign orders from thy nostrills went,
For our accounts the waters were affraid,
Perceivd thy presence & together fled,
In heaps uprightly placd they learnd to stand,
Like banks of Christall by ye paths of sand.
Then fondly flushd with hope, & swelld with pride,
& filld with rage, the foe prophanely cryd,
Secure of conquest Ile pursue their way,
Ile overtake them, Ile divide the prey,
My lust I'le Satisfy, mine anger cloy,
My sword Ile brandish, & their name destroy.
How wildly threats their anger: hark above
New blasts of wind on new commission move,
To loose the fetters that confind the main,
& make its mighty waters rage again,
Then overwhelmd with irresistless Sway
They Sunk like lead they sunk beneath the Sea.

O who like thee thou dreaded Lord of Host
Among the Gods whom all the nations boast
Such acts of wonder & of Strength displays,
O Great! O Glorious in thine holy ways!
Deserving praise, & that thy praise appear
In Signs of reverence & Sence of fear.
With Justice armd thou stretcht thy powrfull hand,
& earth between its gaping Jaws of land,
Receivd its waters of the parted main,
& swallowd up the dark Ægyptian train.
With mercy rising on the weaker Side,
Thy self became the rescud peoples guide,
& in thy strength they past th' amazing road,
To reach thine holy mount thy blessd abode.

What thou hast don the neighb'ring realms shall hear,
& feel the strange report excite their fear.
What thou hast don shall Edoms Dukes amaze,
& make dispair on Palestina Seize.
Shall make the warlike Sons of Moab Shake,
& all the melting hearts of Canaan weak.
In heavy damps diffusd on ev'ry breast
Shall cold distrust & hopeless Terrour rest.
The matchless greatness which thine hand has shown,
Shall keep their kingdomes as unmovd as stone,
While Jordan Stops above & failes below,
& all thy flock across the Channel go.
Thus on thy mercys silver-shining wing
Through seas & streams thou wilt ye nation bring,
& as the rooted trees securely stand,

So firmly plant it in the promisd land,
Where for thy self thou wilt a place prepare,
& after-ages will thine altar rear.
There reign victorious in thy Sacred Seat,
O Lord for ever & for ever great.

Look where the Tyrant was but lately seen,
The Seas gave backward & he venturd in,
In yonder gulph with haughty pomp he showd,
Here marchd his horsemen, there his chariots rode;
& when our God restord the floods again,
Ah vainly strong they perishd in the main.
But Israel went a dry surprizing way,
Made safe by miracles amidst ye sea.

Here ceasd the Song, tho' not ye Prophets Joy,
Which others hands & others tongues employ.
For still the lays with warmth divine expresst
Inflamd his hearers to their inmost breast.
Then Miriams notes the Chorus sweetly raise,
& Miriams timbrel gives new life to praise.
The moving sounds, like Soft delicious wind
That breathd from Paradise, a passage find,
Shed Sympathys for Odours as they rove,
& fan the risings of enkindled love.
Ore all ye crowd the thought inspiring flew,
The women followd with their timbrells too,
& thus from Moses where his strains arose,
They catchd a rapture to perform the close.

We'le sing to God, we'le sing ye songs of praise
To God triumphant in his wondrous ways,
To God whose glorys in ye Seas excell,
Where ye proud horse & prouder rider fell.

Thus Israel rapturd wth ye pleasing thought
Of Freedome wishd & wonderfully gott,
Made chearfull thanks from evry bank rebound,
Expressd by songs, improvd in Joy by sound.

O Sacred Moses, each infusing line
That movd their gratitude was part of thine,
& still the Christians in thy numbers view,
The type of Baptism & of Heaven too.
So Soules from water rise to Grace below:
So Saints from toil to praise & glory goe.

O gratefull Miriam in thy temper wrought
too warm for Silence or inventing thought
Thy part of anthem was to warble o're
In sweet response what Moses sung before.

Thou led the publick voice to Joyn his lays,
& words redoubling well redoubled praise.
Receive thy title, Prophetess was thine
When here thy Practice showd ye form divine.
The Spirit thus approvd, resignd in will
The Church bows down, & hears responses still.

Nor slightly suffer tunefull Jubals name
To miss his place among ye Sons of Fame,
Whose Sweet infusions coud of old inspire,
The breathing organs & ye trembling Lyre.
Father of these on earth, whose gentle Soul
By such ingagements coud ye mind controul,
If holy verses ought to Musick owe,
Be that thy large account of thanks below,
Whilst then ye timbrels lively pleasure gave,
& now whilst organs Sound Sedately grave.

My first attempt ye finishd course commends,
Now Fancy flagg not as that subject ends,
But charmd with beautys which attend thy way,
Ascend harmonious in the next essay.
So flys ye Lark, (& learn from her to fly)
She mounts, she warbles in ye wind on high,
She falls from thence, & seems to drop her wing,
but e're she lights to rest remounts to sing.

It is not farr the days have rolld their years,
Before the Second brightend work appears.
It is not farr, Alas the faulty cause
Which from the Prophet sad reflection draws!
Alas that blessings in possession cloy,
& peevish murmurs are preferrd to Joy,
That favourd Israel coud be faithless still,
& question Gods protecting power or will,
Or dread devoted Canaans warlike men,
& Long for Ægypt & their bonds again.

Scarce thrice the Sun since hardend Pharaoh dyd
As bridegrooms issue forth with glitt'ring pride
Rejoycing rose, & lett ye nation See
Three Shining days of easy liberty,
Ere the mean fears of want producd within
Vain thought replenishd with rebellious Sin.
O Look not Israel to thy former way,
God cannot fail, & either wait or pray.
Within the borders of thy promisd Lands,
Lots hapless wife a strange example stands,
She turnd her eyes & felt her change begin,
& wrath as fierce may meet resembling Sin.
Then forward move thy camp & forward Still,

& lett sweet mercy bend thy Stubborn will.

At thy complaint a branch in Marah cast
With sweetning virtue mends ye waters tast.
At thy complaint the Lab'ring Tempest sailes,
& drives afore a wondrous showr of Quailes.
On tender grass the falling Manna lyes,
& Heav'n it self the want of bread supplys.
The rock divided flows upon the plain,
At thy complaint, & still thou wil't complain.
As thus employd thou went ye desart through,
Lo Sinai mount upreard its head to view.
Thine eyes perceivd the darkly-rolling cloud,
Thine ears the trumpet shrill ye thunder loud,
The forky lightning shot in livid gleam,
The Smoke arose, ye mountain all aflame
Quak'd to ye depths, & worked with signs of awe,
While God descended to dispense the law.
Yet neither mercy manifest in might
Nor pow'r in terrour coud preserve thee right.

Provokt with crimes of such an heinous kind
Allmighty Justice sware the doom designd,
That these shoud never reach ye promisd seat,
& Moses gently mourns their hastend fate.

Ile think him now resignd to publick care,
While night on pitchy plumes slides soft in air.
Ile think him giving what ye guilty sleep
To thoughts where Sorrow glides & numbers weep,
Sad thoughts of woes that reign where Sins prevail,
& mans short life, tho' not so short as frail.
Within this circle for his inward eyes
He bids the fading low creation rise,
& streight a train of mimick Senses brings
The dusky shapes of transitory things,
Thro' pensive shades the visions seem to range,
They seem to flourish, & they seem to change;
A moon decreasing runs the silent sky,
The sickly birds on molting feathers fly,
Men walking count their days of blessings o're,
The blessings vanish & the tales no more,
Still hours of nightly watches steal away,
Big waters roll green blades of grass decay,
Then all ye Pensive shades by Just degrees
Grows faint confuses & goes off with these.
But while the affecting notions pass along,
He chuses such as best adorn his song,
& thus with God the rising lays began,
God ever reigning God, compard with man:
& thus they movd to man beneath his rod;

Man deeply sinning, man chastisd by God.

O Lord O Saviour, tho' thy chosen band
Have staid like strangers in a forreign land,
Through numberd ages which have run their race,
Still has thy mercy been our dwelling place.
Before the most exalted dust of earth,
The stately mountains had receivd a birth;
Before the pillars of the world were laid,
Before its habitable parts were made,
Thou wer't the God, from thee their rise they drew,
Thou great for ages great for ever too.

Man (mortall creature framd to feel decays)
Thine unresisted pow'r at pleasure sways,
Thou sayst return & parting Soules obey,
Thou sayst return & bodys fall to clay.
For whats a thousand fleeting years wth thee?
Or Time compard with long eternity,
Whose wings expanding infinitely vast,
Orestretch its utmost ends of first & last?
Tis like those hours that lately saw ye Sun,
He rose, & set, & all the day was don.
Or like the watches which dead night divide,
& while we slumber unregarded glide,
Where all ye present seems a thing of nought,
& past & future close to waking thought.

As raging floods, when rivers swell with rain,
Bear down ye groves & overflow ye plain,
So swift & strong thy wondrous might appears,
So Life is carryd down the rolling years.
As heavy sleep pursues the days retreat,
With dark with silent & unactive state,
So lifes attended on by certain doom,
& deaths ye rest, ye resting place a tomb.
It quickly rises & it guickly goes,
& youth its morning, age its evening shows.
Thus tender blades of grass, when beams diffuse,
Rise from the pressure of their early dews,
Point tow'rds ye skys their elevated spires,
& proudly flourish in their green attires,
But soon (ah fading state of things below!)
The Scyth destructive mows ye lovely show,
The rising Sun that Saw their glorys high
That Sun descending sees their glorys dy.

We still with more than common hast of fate
Are doomd to perish in thy kindled hate.
Our publick sins for publick Justice call,
& stand like markes on which thy Judgements fall.

Our secret sins that folly thought conceald
Are in thy light for punishment reveald.
Beneath the terrours of thy wrath divine
Our days unmixd with happiness decline,
Like empty storys tedious, short, & vain,
& never never more recalld again.

Yet what were Life, if to ye longest date
Which men have namd a life we backned fate?
Alas its most computed length appears
To reach ye limits but of Seav'nty years,
& if by strength to fourscore years we goe,
That strength is labour, & that labour woe.
Then will thy term expire, & thou must fly
O man O Creature surely born to dy.

But who regards a truth so throughly known?
Who dreads a wrath so manifestly shown?
Who seems to fear it tho' ye danger vyes
With any pitch to which our fear can rise?
O teach us so to number all our days
That these reflections may correct our ways,
That these may lead us from delusive dreams
To walk in heavnly wisdomes golden beams.

Return O Lord, how Long shall Israels sin
How Long thine anger be preservd within!
Before our times irrevocably past
Be kind be gracious & return at last.
Let Favour soon-dispensd our soules employ,
& long endure to make enduring Joy.
Send years of comforts for our years of woes,
Send these at least of equall length with those.
Shine on thy flock & on their offspring shine
With tender mercy (sweetest act divine).
Bright rays of Majesty serenely shed,
To rest in Glorys on the nations head.
Our future deeds with approbation bless,
& in the giving them give us success.

Thus with forgiveness earnestly desird,
Thus in the raptures of a bliss requird,
The man of God concludes his Sacred Strain,
Now sitt & see ye subject once again.

See Ghastly Death where Desarts all around
Spread forth their barren undelightfull ground:
There stalks the silent melancholly shade,
His naked bones reclining on a spade,
& thrice the spade with solemn sadness heaves,
& thrice earth opens in the form of graves,

His gates of darkness gape to take him in,
Then where he soon woud Sink he's pushed by sin.

Poor Mortalls here your common picture know,
& with your Selves in this acquainted grow.
Through life with airy thoughtless pride you range
& vainly glitter in the Sphear of change,
A sphear where all things but for time remain,
Where no fixd starrs with endless glory reign,
But Meteors onely short-lived Meteors rise
To shine shoot down & dy beneath ye skys.

There is an hour, Ah who yt hour attends!
When man ye guilded vanity descends.
When forreign force or wast of inward heat
Constrain ye soul to leave its ancient seat;
When banishd Beauty from her empire flyes,
& with a languish leaves ye Sparkling eyes;
When softning Musick & Persuasion fail,
& all the charms that in ye tongue prevail,
When Spirits stop their course, when nerves unbrace,
& outward action & perception cease.
'Tis then the poor deformd remains shall be
That naked Skeleton we seem to see.

Make this thy mirrour if thou woudst have bliss,
No flattring image shows it self in this;
But such as lays the lofty lookes of pride,
& makes cool thought in humble channel glide;
But such as clears ye cheats of Errours den,
Whence magick mists surround ye soules of men,
Whence Self-Delusions trains adorn their flight,
As Snows fair feathers fleet to darken sight,
Then rest, & in the work of Fancy spread
To gay-wavd plumes for ev'ry mortals head.
These empty Forms when Death appears disperse,
Or melt in tears upon its mournfull hearse,
The sad reflection forces men to know,
"Life surely failes & swiftly flys below.

O Least thy folly loose ye proffit sought
O never touch it with a glancing thought,
As men to glasses come, & straight wth draw,
& straight forgett what sort of face they saw:
But fix intently fix thine inward eyes,
& in the strength of this great truth be wise.
"If on ye globes dim Side our sences Stray,
"Not usd to perfect light we think it day:
"Death seems long sleep, & hopes of heavnly beams
"Deceitfull wishes big with distant dreams.
"But if our reason purge ye carnal sight,

"& place its objects in their Juster light,
"We change ye side, from Dreams on earth we move,
"& wake through death to rise in life above.

Here ore my soul a solemn silence reigns,
Preparing thought for new celestial strains.
The former vanish off, ye new begin,
The solemn silence stands like night between,
In whose dark bosome day departing lyes,
& day succeeding takes a lovely rise.
But tho' ye song be changd, be still ye flame,
& Still ye prophet in my lines ye Same,
With care renewd upon the children dwell,
Whose sinfull Fathers in the desart fell,
With care renewd (if any care can do)
Ah least they sin & least they perish too.

Go seek for Moses at yon Sacred tent
On which ye Presence makes a bright descent.
Behold ye cloud with radiant glory fair
Like a wreathd pillar curl its gold in air.
Behold it hovering Just above the door,
& Moses meekely kneeling on the floor.
But if the gazing turn thine edge of sight,
& darkness Spring from unsupported light,
Then change ye Sense, be sight in hearing drownd,
While these strange accents from the vision sound.
The time my Servant is approaching nigh
When thou shall't gatherd with thy Fathers ly,
& soon thy nation quite forgetfull grown
Of all the glorys which mine arm has shown,
Shall through my covenant perversely break,
Despise my worship & my name forsake,
By customes conquerd where to rule they go,
& Serving Gods that cant protect ye foe.
Displeasd at this Ile turn my face aside
Till sharp Afflictions rod reduce their pride
Till brought to better mind they seek relief,
by good confessions in the midst of grief.
Then write thy song to stand a witness still
Of favours past & of my future will,
For I their vain conceits before discern,
Then write thy Song which Israels sons shall learn.

As thus ye wondrous voice its charge repeats
The Prophet musing deep within retreats.
He Seems to feel it on a streaming ray
Pierce through ye Soul enlightning all its way.
& much Obedient will & free desire,
& much his Love of Jacobs Seed inspire,
& much O much above ye warmth of those

The Sacred Spirit in his bosome glows,
Majestick Notion Seems Decrees to nod,
& Holy Transport speakes ye words of God.

Returnd at length, the finishd roll he brings,
Enrichd with Strains of past & future things.
The Priests in order to ye tent repair,
The Gatherd Tribes attend their Elders there:
O Sacred Mercys inexhausted Store!
Shall these have warning of their faults before,
Shall these be told ye recompenses due,
Shall Heavn & Earth be calld to witness too!
Then still ye tumult if it will be so,
Its Fear to loose a word lett caution Show,
Lett close Attention in dead calm appear,
& softly softly steal with silence near,
While Moses raisd above ye listning throng,
Pronounces thus in all their ears the Song.

Hear O ye Heav'ns Creations lofty show,
Hear O thou heavn-encompassd Earth below.
As Silver Showrs of gently-dropping rain,
As Honyd Dews distilling on ye plain,
As rain as Dews for tender grass designd,
So shall my speeches sink within ye mind,
So sweetly turn ye Soules enlivening food,
So fill & cherish hopefull seeds of good.
For now my Numbers to the world Abroad,
Will lowdly celebrate ye name of God.

Ascribe thou nation, evry favour'd tribe
Excelling greatness to ye Lord ascribe,
The Lord, the Rock on whom we safely trust,
Whose work is perfect, & whose ways are Just,
The Lord whose promise stands for ever true,
The Lord most righteous & most holy too.

Ah worse Election! Ah the bonds of sin!
They chuse themselves to take corruption in.
They stain their soules with vices deepest blots,
When onely frailtys are his childrens spots.
Their thoughts words actions all are run astray,
& none more crooked more perverse than they.

Say rebell Nation O unwisely light,
Say will thy folly thus thy God requite?
Or is He not the God who made thee free,
Whose mercy purchasd & establishd thee?

Remember well ye wondrous days of old,
The years of ages long before thee told,

Ask all thy fathers who the truth will show,
Or ask thine elders for thine elders know.

When ye most high with scepter pointed down
Describd ye Realms of each beginning Crown,
When Adams offspring Providentiall care
To people countrys scatterd here & there,
He so ye limits of their lands confind,
That favourd Israel has its part assignd,
For Israel is ye Lords, & gaines ye place
Reservd for those whom he woud chuse to grace.

Him in ye desart him his mercy found
Where famine dwells & howling deafs ye ground,
Where dread is felt by savage noise encreast,
Where solitude erects its seat on wast.
& there he led him, & he taught him there,
& safely kept him with a watchfull care,
The tender apples of our heedfull eye
Not more in guard nor more securely ly.
& as an eagle that attempts to bring
Her unexperiencd young to trust the wing,
Stirrs up her nest, & flutters ore their heads,
& all ye forces of her pinnions spreads,
& takes & bears ym on her plumes above,
To give peculiar proof of royall love,
Twas so ye Lord, the gracious Lord alone,
With kindness most peculiar led his own,
As no strange God concurrd to make him free,
So none had powr to lead him through but he.
To lands excelling lands & planted high
That boast ye kindlyest-influencing sky
He brought, he bore him on ye wings of Grace,
To tast ye plentys of ye grounds encrease,
Sweet-dropping hony from the rocky soil,
From flinty rocks ye smoothly-flowing oyl,
The guilded butter from the stately kine,
The milk with which ye duggs of sheep decline,
The marrow-fatness of the tender lambs,
The bulky breed of Basans goats & rams,
The finest flowry wheat that crowns the plain
Distends its husk & loads the blade with grain,
& still he drank from ripe delicious heaps
Of clusters pressd the purest blood of grapes.

But thou art waxen fatt & kickest now,
O Well-Directed O Jesurun thou.
Thou soon w'ert fatt, thy sides were thickly grown,
Thy fattness deeply coverd evry bone
Then wanton fullness vain oblivion brought,
& God that made & savd thee was forgott,

While Gods of forreign lands & rites abhorrd,
To Jealousys & anger movd ye Lord;
While Gods thy fathers never knew were ownd;
& Hell ev'n Hell with sacrifice attond.
Oh fooles unmindfull whence your orderd frame
& whence your life-infusing spirit came!
Such strange corruptions his revenge provoke,
& thus their fate his indignation spoke.

It is decreed. Ile hide my face & see
When I forsake them what their end shall be.
For they're a froward very froward strain,
That promisd duty but returnd disdain.
In my grievd soul they raise a Jealous flame
By new-namd Gods & onely Gods in name,
They make the burnings of mine anger glow
By guilty vanitys displeasing show:
Ile also teach their Jealousy to frett
At people not formd a people yet,
Ile make their anger vex their inward breast
When such as have not known my laws are blesst.
A fire a fire that nothing can asswage
Is kindled in the fierceness of my rage,
To burn the deeps, consume ye lands increase,
& on the mountains strong foundations seize.
Thick heaps of mischief on their heads I send,
& all mine arrows wingd with fury spend.
Slow-parching dearth & pestilentiall heat,
Shall bring the bitter pangs of lingring fate.
Sharp teeth of beasts shall swift destruction bring,
Dire serpents wound them with invenomd sting,
The sword without & dread within consume
The youth the virgin in their lovely bloom,
Weak tender Infancy by suckling fed,
& helpless age with hoary-frosted head.
I said Ide scatter all the sinfull race,
I said Ide make its meer remembrance cease,
But much I feard the foes unruly pride,
Their glory vaunted & my powr denyd,
While thus they boast, our arm has shown us brave,
& God did nothing, for he could not Save.
So fond their thought, so farr remote of sense,
& blind in every course of Providence.
O knew they rightly where my Judgements tend,
O woud they ponder on their latter end!
Soon woud they find, that when upon ye field
One makes a thousand two ten thousand yield,
The Lord of Hosts has Sold a rebel state,
The Lord inclosd it in ye netts of fate.
For whats anothers rock compard with ours,
Lett them be Judges that have provd their powrs,

That on their own have vainly calld for aid,
While ours to freedome & to glory led.
Their vine may seem indeed to flourish fair,
But yet it grows in Sodoms tainted air,
It sucks corruption from Gomorrahs fields,
Rank Galls for grapes in bitter clusters yields,
& poison sheds for wine, like yt which comes
From asps & Dragons death-infected gums;
& are not these their hatefull sins reveald,
& in my treasures for my Justice seald?
To me the province of revenge belongs,
To me the certain recompense of wrongs,
Their feet shall totter in appointed time,
& threatning danger overtake their crime,
For wingd with featherd hast ye minutes fly,
To bring those things that must afflict them nigh.
The Lord will Judge his own & bring ym low,
& then repent & turn upon ye foe,
& when the Judgements from his own remove,
Will thus the foe convincingly reprove.
Where are ye Gods ye rock to whom in vain
Your offrings have been made your victims slain?
Lett them arise, lett them afford their aid,
& with Protections shield surround your head.
Know then your maker, I the Lord am he,
Nor ever was there any God with me,
& death or life & wounds or health I give,
Nor can another from my powr reprieve.
With Solemn state I lift mine arm on high
Ore ye rich glorys of the lofty sky,
& by my self majestically swear,
I live for ever & for ever there.
If in my rage ye glitt'ring sword I whet,
& sternly sitting take ye Judgement seat,
My Just-awarding sentence dooms my foe,
& vengeance wields ye blade & gives ye blow,
& Deep in flesh ye blade of Fury bites,
& deadly-deep my bearded arrow lightes,
& both grow drunk with blood defild in sin,
When executions of revenge begin.

Then lett his nation in a common voice,
& with his nation lett ye world rejoyce.
For whether God for crimes or tryalls spill
His Servants blood, he will avenge it still.
He'le break ye troops, he'le scatter all afarr
Who vex our realm with desolating warr.
& on ye favour tribes & on their land
Shed Victorys & peace from Mercys hand.

Here ceasd ye song, & Israel lookd behind

& gazd before with unconfining mind,
& fixd in silence & amazement saw
The strokes of all their state beneath ye law.
Their Recollection does its light present
To show ye mountain blessd with Gods descent,
To show their wandrings, their unfixd abode,
& all their guidance in the desert road.
Then where the beams of Recollection goe
To leave ye fancy dispossessd of show,
The fairer light of Prophecy's begun
Which opening future days supplys their sun.
By such a sun (& fancy needs no more)
They see the coming times & walk ym o're,
& now they gain that rest their travel sought,
Now milk & hony stream along the thought,
Anon they fill their soules, ye blessings cloy,
& God's forgot in full excess of Joy.
& oft they sin, & oft his anger burns
& ev'ry nations made their scourge by turns,
Till oft repenting they convert to God,
& he repenting too destroys the rod.

O nation timely warnd in sacred strain,
O never lett thy Moses sing in vain.
Dare to be good & happiness prolong
Or if thy folly will fullfill the song,
At least be found the seldomer in ill,
& still repent & soon repent thee still.
When such fair paths thou shalt avoid to tread,
Thy blood will rest upon thy sinfull head,
Thy crime by lasting long secure thy foe,
The gracious warning to the Gentiles goe,
& all the world thats calld to witness here
Convincd by thine example learn to fear.
The gentil world a mystick Israel grown
Will in thy first condition find their own,
A Gods descent, a Pilgrimage below,
& Promisd rest where living waters flow.
They'le see the pen describe in ev'ry trace,
The frowns of Anger, or the Smiles of Grace,
Why mercy turns aside & leaves to shine,
What cause provokes the Jealousy divine,
Why Justice kindles dire-avenging flames,
What endless powr ye Lifted Arm proclaims,
Why Mercy shines again with chearfull ray,
& Glory double-gilds ye lightsome day.
Tho Nations change & Israels empire dyes,
Yet still ye case which rose before may rise,
Eternall Providence its rule retains,
& still preserves, & still applys ye strains.

Twas such a gift ye Prophets sacred pen
On his departure left ye sons of men.
Thus he, & thus ye Swan her breath resigns
(Within ye beautys of Poetick lines,)
He white with innocence, his figure she,
& both harmonious, but the sweeter he.
Death learns to charm, & while it leads to bliss
Has found a lovely circumstance in this
To suit the meekest turn of easy mind,
& actions chearfull in an air resignd.

Thou flock whom Moses to thy freedome led
How will't thou lay the venerable dead?
Go (if thy Fathers taught a work they knew)
Go build a Pyramid to Glory due,
Square ye broad base, with sloping sides arise,
& lett the point diminish in the skys.
There leave the corps, suspending ore his head
The wand whose motion winds & waves obeyd.
On Sabled Banners to ye sight describe
The painted arms of evry mourning tribe,
& thus may publick grief adorn ye tomb
Deep-streaming downwards through ye vaulted room.
On the black stone a fair inscription raise
That Sums his Government to speak his praise,
& may the style as brightly worth proclaim,
As if Affection with a pointed beam
Engravd or fird ye words, or Honour due
Had with its self inlaid ye tablet through.

But stop ye pomp that is not mans to pay,
For God will grace him in a nobler way.
Mine eyes perceive an orb of heavnly state
With splendid forms & light serene repleat,
I hear the Sound of fluttring wings in air,
I hear the tunefull tongues of Angels there,
They fly, they bear, they rest on Nebo's head,
& in thick glory wrap the rev'rend dead.
This errand crowns his songs, & tends to prove
His near communion with ye quire above.
Now swiftly down the Steepy mount they go,
Now swiftly glides their shining orb below,
& now moves off where rising grounds deny
To spread their vally to the distant eye.
Ye blessd inhabitants of glitt'ring air
You've born ye prophet but we know not where.
Perhaps least Israel overfondly led
In rating worth when envy leaves ye dead,
Might plant a grove, invent new rites divine,
Make him their Idol, & his grave ye shrine.

But what disorder? what repells ye light
& ere its season forces up ye night?
Why sweep the spectres ore ye blasted ground?
What shakes ye mount with hollow-roaring sound?
Hell rolls beneath it, Terrour stalkes before
With shriekes & groans, & Horrour bursts a door,
& Satan rises in infernall state
Drawn up by Malice Envy Rage & Hate.
A darkning Vapour with sulphureous steam,
In pitchy curlings, edgd by sullen flame,
& framd a chariot for ye dreadfull Form,
Drives whirling up on mad Confusions storm.

Then fiercely turning where ye Prophet dyd,
Nor shall thy nation scape my wrath he cry'd;
This corps Ile enter & thy flock mislead,
& all thy Miracles my lyes shall aid.
But where?—Hes gon, & by ye scented sky
The fav'rite courtiers have been lately nigh.
O slow to buisness, cursd in mischiefs hour,
Track on their Odours, & if Hell has powr—
This said with spight & with a bent for ill
He shot in fury from ye trembling hill.

In vain Proud Fiend thy threats are half exprest,
& half ly choaking in thy scornfull breast,
His shining bearers have performd ye rite,
& laid him softly down in shades of night.
A Warriour heads ye band, Great Michael he,
Renownd for conquest in ye warr with thee,
A sword of flame to stop thy course he bears,
Nor has thy rage availd, nor can thy snares,
The Lord rebuke thy pride he meekly cryes:
The Lord has heard him & thy project dyes.

Here Moses leaves my song, ye tribes retire,
The desart flyes, & fourty years expire.
& now my fancy for awhile be still,
& think of coming down from Nebo's hill.
Go Search among thy forms, & thence prepare
A cloud in folds of Soft-surrounding air,
Go find a breeze to lift thy cloud on high,
To waft thee gently rockd in open sky,
Then stealing back to leave a silent calm,
& thee reposing in a grove of palm.
The place will suit my next-succeeding strain,
& Ile awake thee soon to sing again.

To Henry, Lord Viscount Bolingbroke.

I hate the Vulgar with untuneful Mind,
Hearts uninspir'd, and Senses unrefin'd.
Hence ye Prophane, I raise the sounding String,
And Bolingbroke descends to hear me sing.

When Greece cou'd Truth in Mystick Fable shroud,
And with Delight instruct the list'ning Crowd,
An ancient Poet (Time has lost his Name)
Deliver'd Strains on Verse to future Fame.
Still as he sung he touch'd the trembling Lyre,
And felt the Notes a rising Warmth inspire.
Ye sweet'ning Graces in the Musick Throng,
Assist my Genius, and retrieve the Song
From dark Oblivion. See, my Genius goes
To call it forth. 'Twas thus the Poem rose.

Wit is the Muses Horse, and bears on high
The daring Rider to the Muses Sky:
Who, while his strength to mount aloft he tries,
By Regions varying in their Nature, flies.

At first he riseth o'er a Land of Toil,
A barren, hard, and undeserving Soil,
Where only Weeds from heavy Labour grow,
Which yet the Nation prune, and keep for show.
Where Couplets jingling on their Accent run,
Whose point of Epigram is sunk to Pun.
Where Wings by Fancy never feather'd fly,
Where Lines by measure form'd in Hatchets lie;
Where Altars stand, erected Porches gape,
And Sense is cramp'd while Words are par'd to shape;
Where mean Acrosticks labour'd in a Frame,
On scatter'd Letters raise a painful Scheme;
And by Confinement in their Work controul
The great Enlargings of the boundless Soul.
Where if a Warriour's elevated Fire
Wou'd all the brightest Strokes of Verse require,
Then streight in Anagram a wretched Crew
Will pay their undeserving Praises too;
While on the rack his poor disjointed Name
Must tell its Master's Character to Fame.
And (if my Fire and Fears aright presage)
The lab'ring Writers of a future Age
Shall clear new ground, and Grotts and Caves repair,
To civilize the babbling Ecchoes there.
Then while a Lover treads a lonely Walk,
His Voice shall with its own Reflection talk,
The closing Sounds of all the vain Device,

Select by trouble frivolously nice,
Resound through Verse, and with a false Pretence
Support the Dialogue, and pass for Sense.
Can things like these to lasting Praise pretend?
Can any Muse the worthless Toil befriend?
Ye sacred Virgins, in my Thoughts ador'd,
Ah, be for ever in my Lines deplor'd!
If Tricks on Words acquire an endless Name,
And Trifles merit in the Court of Fame.

'At this the Poet stood concern'd a while,
'And view'd his Objects with a scornful Smile:
'Then other Images of diff'rent kind,
'With diff'rent Workings enter'd on his Mind;
'At whose Approach he felt the former gone,
'And shiver'd in Conceit, and thus went on.

By a cold Region next the Rider goes,
Where all lies cover'd in eternal Snows;
Where no bright Genius drives the Chariot high,
To glitter on the Ground, and gild the Sky.
Bleak level Realm, where Frigid Stiles abound,
Where never yet a daring Thought was found,
But counted Feet is Poetry defin'd;
And starv'd Conceits that chill the Reader's Mind
A little Sense in many Words imply,
And drag with loit'ring numbers slowly by.
Here dry sententious Speeches half asleep,
Prolong'd in Lines, o'er many Pages creep;
Nor ever shew the Passions well exprest,
Nor raise like Passions in another's Breast.
Here flat Narrations fair Exploits debase,
In Measures void of ev'ry shining Grace;
Which never arm their Hero for the Field,
Nor with Prophetick Story paint the Shield,
Nor fix the Crest, or make the Feathers wave,
Or with their Characters reward the Brave;
Undeck'd they stand, and unadorn'd with Praise,
And fail to profit while they fail to please.
Here forc'd Description is so strangely wrought,
It never stamps its Image on the Thought;
The liveless Trees may stand for ever bare,
And Rivers stop, for ought the Readers care;
They see no Branches trembling in the Woods,
Nor hear the Murmurs of encreasing Floods,
Which near the Roots with ruffled Waters flow,
And shake the shadows of the Boughs below.
Ah sacred Verse, replete with heav'nly Flame,
Such cold Endeavours wou'd invade thy Name!
The Writer fondly wou'd in these survive,
Which wanting Spirit never seem'd alive:

But if Applause or Fame attend his Pen,
Let breathless Statues pass for breathing Men.

'Here seem'd the Singer touch'd at what he sung,
'And Grief a while delay'd his Hand and Tongue:
'But soon he check'd his Fingers, chose a Strain,
'And flourish'd shrill, and thus arose again.

Pass the next Region which appears to show,
'Tis very open, unimprov'd, and low;
No noble Flights of elevated Thought,
No nervous strength of Sense maturely wrought,
Possess this Realm; but common Turns are there,
Which idely sportive move with childish Air.
On callow Wings, and like a Plague of Flies,
The little Fancies in a Poem rise,
The jaded Reader ev'ry where to strike,
And move his Passions ev'ry where alike.
There all the graceful Nymphs are forc'd to play
Where any Water bubbles in the way:
There shaggy Satyrs are oblig'd to rove
In all the Fields, and over all the Grove:
There ev'ry Star is summon'd from its Sphear,
To dress one Face, and make Clorinda fair:
There Cupids fling their Darts in ev'ry Song,
While Nature stands neglected all along:
Till the teiz'd Hearer, vex'd at last to find
One constant Object still assault the Mind,
Admires no more at what's no longer new,
And hastes to shun the persecuting View.
There bright Surprizes of Poetick Rage,
(Whose Strength and Beauty more confirm'd in Age
For having lasted, last the longer still)
By weak Attempts are imitated ill,
Or carry'd on beyond their proper Light,
Or with Refinement flourish'd out of sight.
There Metaphors on Metaphors abound,
And Sense by differing Images confound:
Strange injudicious Management of Thought,
Not born to Rage, nor into Method brought.
Ah, sacred Muse! from such a Realm retreat,
Nor idly waste the Infl'ence of thy Heat
On shallow Soils, where quick Productions rise,
And wither as the Warmth that rais'd them dies.

'Here o'er his Breast a sort of Pity roll'd,
'Which something lab'ring in the Mind controul'd,
'And made him touch the loud-resounding Strings,
'While thus with Musick's stronger Tones he sings.

Mount higher still, still keep thy faithful Seat,

Mind the firm Reins, and curb thy Courser's Heat;
Nor let him touch the Realms that next appear,
Whose hanging Turrets seem a Fall to fear,
And strangely stand along the Tracts of Air
Where Thunder rolls, and bearded Comets glare.
The Thoughts that most extravagantly soar,
The Words that sound as if they meant to roar;
For Rant and Noise are offer'd here to Choice,
And stand elected by the Publick Voice.
All Schemes are slighted which attempt to shine
At once with strange and probable Design;
'Tis here a mean Conceit, a vulgar View,
That bears the least Respect to seeming true;
While ev'ry trifling turn of things is seen
To move by Gods descending in Machine.
Here swelling Lines with stalking Strut proceed,
And in the Clouds terrifick Rumblings breed:
Here single Heroes deal grim Deaths around,
And Armies perish in tremendous Sound:
Here fearful Monsters are preserv'd to die,
In such a Tumult as affrights the Sky;
For which the Golden Sun shall hide with dread,
And Neptune lift his sedgy-matted Head,
Admire the Roar, and dive with dire Dismay,
And seek his deepest Chambers in the Sea.
To raise their Subject thus the Lines devise,
And false Extravagance wou'd fain surprize;
Yet still, ye Gods, ye live untouch'd by Fear,
And undisturb'd at bellowing Monsters here:
But with Compassion guard the Brain of Men,
If thus they bellow through the Poet's Pen:
So will the Readers Eyes discern aright
The rashest Sally from the noblest Flight,
And find that only Boast and Sound agree
To seem the Life and Voice of Majesty,
When writers rampant on Apollo call,
And bid him enter and possess them all,
And make his Flames afford a wild Pretence
To keep them unrestrain'd by common Sense.
Ah, sacred Verse! lest Reason quit thy Seat,
Give none to such, or give a gentler Heat.

''Twas here the Singer felt his Temper wrought
'By fairer Prospects, which arose to Thought;
'And in himself a while collected sat,
'And much admir'd at this, and much at that;
'Till all the beauteous Forms in order ran,
'And then he took their Track, and thus began.

Above the Beauties, far above the Show
In which weak Nature dresses here below,

Stands the great Palace of the Bright and Fine,
Where fair Ideas in full Glory shine,
Eternal Models of exalted Parts,
The Pride of Minds, and Conquerors of Hearts.

Upon the first Arrival here, are seen
Rang'd Walks of Bay, the Muses ever-Green,
Each sweetly springing from some sacred Bough,
Whose circling Shade adorn'd a Poet's Brow,
While through the Leaves, in unmolested Skies,
The gentle breathing of Applauses flies,
And flatt'ring Sounds are heard within the Breeze,
And pleasing Murmur runs among the Trees,
And falls of Water join the flatt'ring Sounds,
And Murmur soft'ning from the Shore rebounds.
The warbled Melody, the lovely Sights,
The Calms of Solitude inspire Delights,
The dazzled Eyes, the ravish'd Ears, are caught,
The panting Heart unites to purer Thought,
And grateful Shiverings wander o'er the Skin,
And wondrous Ecstasies arise within,
Whence Admiration overflows the Mind,
And leaves the Pleasure felt, but undefin'd.
Stay, daring Rider, now no longer rove;
Now pass to find the Palace through the Grove;
Whate'er you see, whate'er you feel, display
The Realm you sought for, daring Rider stay.

Here various Fancy spreads a vary'd Scene,
And Judgment likes the sight, and looks serene,
And can be pleas'd its self, and helps to please,
And joins the Work, and regulates the Lays.
Thus on a Plan, design'd by double Care,
The Building rises in the glittering Air,
With just Agreement fram'd in ev'ry part,
And smoothly polish'd with the nicest Art.

Here Lawrel-boughs, which ancient Heroes wore,
Now not so fading as they prov'd before,
Wreath round the Pillars which the Poets rear,
And slope their Points to make a Foliage there.
Here Chaplets pull'd in gently-breathing Wind,
And wrought by Lovers innocently kind,
Hung o'er the Porch, their fragrant Odours give,
And fresh in lasting Song for ever live.
The Shades, for whom with such indulgent care
Fame wreaths the Boughs or hangs the Chaplets there,
To deathless Honours thus preserv'd above,
For Ages conquer, or for Ages love.

Here bold Description paints the Walls within,

Her Pencil touches, and the World is seen:
The Fields look beauteous in their flow'ry Pride,
The Mountains rear aloft, the Vales subside,
The Cities rise, the Rivers seem to play,
And hanging Rocks repell the foaming Sea;
The foaming Seas their angry Billows show,
Curl'd White above, and darkly roll'd below,
Or cease their Rage, and as they calmly lie,
Return the pleasing Pictures of the Sky;
The Skies extended in an open View,
Appear a lofty distant Arch of Blue,
In which Description stains the painted Bow,
Or thickens Clouds, and feathers out the Snow,
Or mingles Blushes in the Morning ray,
Or gilds the Noon, or turns an Evening gray.

Here on the Pedestalls of War and Peace,
In diff'rent Rows, and with a diff'rent Grace,
Fine Statues proudly ride, or nobly stand,
To which Narration with a pointing Hand
Directs the Sight, and makes Examples please
By boldly vent'ring to dilate in Praise,
While chosen Beauties lengthen out the Song,
Yet make her Hearers never think it long.
Or if with closer Art, with sprightly Mien,
Scarce like her self, and more like Action seen,
She bids their Facts in Images arise,
And seem to pass before the Readers Eyes,
The Words like Charms inchanted Motion give,
And all the Statues of the Palace live.
Then Hosts embattel'd stretch their Lines afar,
Their Leaders Speeches animate the War,
The Trumpets sound, the feather'd Arrows fly,
The Sword is drawn, the Lance is toss'd on high,
The Brave press on, the fainter Forces yield,
And Death in differing Shapes deforms the Field.
Or shou'd the Shepherds be dispos'd to play,
Amintor's jolly Pipe beguiles the Day,
And jocund Ecchoes dally with the Sound,
And Nymphs in measures trip along the ground,
And e're the Dews have wet the Grass below,
Turn homewards singing all the way they go.

Here, as on Circumstance Narrations dwell,
And tell what moves, and hardly seem to tell,
The Toil of Heroes on the dusty Plains,
Or on the Green the Merriment of Swains,
Reflection speaks, then all the Forms that rose
In Life's inchanted Scene themselves compose;
Whilst the grave Voice, controlling all the Spells
With solemn Utt'rance, thus the Moral tells:

So publick worth its Enemies destroys,
Or private innocence it self enjoys.

Here all the Passions, for their greater sway,
In all the Pow'r of Words themselves array;
And hence the soft Pathetick gently charms,
And hence the Bolder fills the Breast with Arms.
Sweet Love in Numbers finds a World of Darts,
And with Desirings wounds the tender Hearts.
Fair Hope displays its Pinnions to the Wind,
And flutters in the Lines, and lifts the Mind.
Brisk Joy with Transport fills the rising Strain,
Breaks in the Notes, and bounds in ev'ry Vein.
Stern Courage, glittering in the sparks of Ire,
Inflames those Lays that set the Breast on fire.
Aversion learns to fly with swifter Will,
In Numbers taught to represent an Ill.
By frightful Accents Fear produces Fears.
By sad Expression Sorrow melts to Tears.
And dire Amazement and Despair are brought
By words of Horror through the Wilds of Thought.
'Tis thus tumultuous Passions learn to roll;
Thus arm'd with Poetry they win the Soul.

Pass further through the Dome, another View
Wou'd now the Pleasures of thy Mind renew,
Where oft Description for the Colours goes,
Which raise and animate its native Shows;
Where oft Narration seeks a florid Grace
To keep from sinking e're 'tis time to cease;
Where easy turns Reflection looks to find,
When Morals aim at Dress to please the Mind;
Where lively Figures are for Use array'd,
And these an Action, those a Passion, aid.

There modest Metaphors in order sit,
With unaffected undisguising Wit,
That leave their own, and seek anothers place,
Not forc'd, but changing with an easy pace,
To deck a Notion faintly seen before,
And Truth preserves her shape, and shines the more.

By these the beauteous Similes reside,
In look more open, in Design ally'd,
Who, fond of Likeness, from anothers Face
Bring ev'ry Feature's corresponding Grace,
With near approaches in Expression flow,
And take the turn their Pattern loves to show;
As in a Glass the Shadows meet the Fair,
And dress and practice with resembling Air.
Thus Truth, by Pleasure doth her Aim pursue,

Looks bright, and fixes on the doubled View.

There Repetitions one another meet,
Expresly strong, or languishingly sweet,
And raise the sort of Sentiment they please,
And urge the sort of Sentiment they raise.

There close in order are the Questions plac'd,
Which march with Art conceal'd in shows of haste,
And work the Reader till his Mind be brought
To make its Answers in the Writers Thought.
For thus the moving Passions seem to throng,
And with their Quickness force the Soul along;
And thus the Soul grows fond they shou'd prevail,
When ev'ry Question seems a fair Appeal;
And if by just degrees of Strength they soar,
In Steps as equal each affects the more.

There strange Commotion naturally shown,
Speaks on regardless that we speak alone,
Nor minds if they to whom she talks be near,
Nor cares if that to which she talks can hear.
The warmth of Anger dares an absent Foe;
The words of Pity speaks to Tears of Woe;
The Love that hopes, on Errands sends the Breeze;
And Love despairing moans to naked Trees.

There stand the new Creations of the Muse,
Poetick Persons, whom the Writers use
Whene'er a Cause magnificently great,
Wou'd fix Attention with peculiar weight.
'Tis hence that humbled Provinces are seen
Transform'd to Matrons with neglected Mien,
Who call their Warriors in a mournful Sound,
And shew their Crowns of Turrets on the ground,
While over Urns reclining Rivers moan
They shou'd enrich a Nation not their own.
'Tis hence the Virtues are no more confin'd
To be but Rules of Reason in the Mind;
Their heav'nly Forms start forth, appear to breath,
And in bright Shapes converse with Men beneath,
And, as a God, in Combat Valour leads,
In Council Prudence as a Goddess aids.

There Exclamations all the Voice employ
In sudden Flushes of Concern or Joy:
Then seem the Sluices which the Passions bound,
To burst asunder with a speechless Sound;
And then with Tumult and Surprize they roul,
And shew the Case important in the Soul.

There rising Sentences attempt to speak,
Which Wonder, Sorrow, Shame, or Anger, break;
But so the Part directs to find the rest,
That what remains behind is more than ghest.
Thus fill'd with Ease, yet left unfinish'd too,
The Sense looks large within the Readers View:
He freely gathers all the Passion means,
And artful Silence more than Words explains.

Methinks a thousand Graces more I see,
And I cou'd dwell—But when wou'd Thought be free?
Engaging Method ranges all the Band,
And smooth Transition joins them hand in hand:
Around the Musick of my Lays they throng,
Ah too deserving Objects of my Song!
Live wondrous Palace, live secure of Time,
To Senses Harmony, to Souls sublime,
And just Proportion all, and great Design,
And lively Colours, and an Air divine.

'Tis here, that guided by the Muses Fire,
And fill'd with sacred Thought, her Friends retire,
Unbent to Care, and unconcern'd with Noise,
To taste Repose and elevated Joys,
Which in a deep untroubled Leisure meet,
Serenely ravishing politely sweet.
From hence the Charms that most engage they choose,
And as they please the glittering Objects use;
While to their Genius more than Art they trust,
Yet Art acknowledges their Labours just.
From hence they look, from this exalted Show,
To choose their Subject in the World below,
And where an Hero well deserves a Name,
They consecrate his Acts in Song to Fame;
Or if a Science unadorn'd they find,
They smooth its Look to please and teach the Mind;
And where a Friendship's generously strong,
They celebrate the Knot of Souls in Song;
Or if the Verses must inflame Desire,
The Thoughts are melted, and the Words on fire:
But when the Temples deck'd with Glory stand,
And Hymns of Gratitude the Gods demand,
Their Bosoms kindle with Celestial Love,
And then alone they cast their Eyes above.
Hail sacred Verse! ye sacred Muses hail!
Cou'd I your Pleasures with your Fire reveal,
The World might then be taught to know you right,
And court your Rage, and envy my Delight.
But whilst I follow where your pointed Beams
My Course directing shoot in golden Streams,
The bright Appearance dazzles Fancy's Eyes,

And weary'd out the fix'd Attention lies,
Enough my Verses have you work'd my Breast,
I'll seek the sacred Grove, and sink to Rest.

'No longer now the ravish'd Poet sung,
'His Voice in easy Cadence left the Tongue;
'Nor o'er the Musick did his Fingers fly,
'The Sounds ran tingling, and they seem'd to die.

O Bolingbroke! O Fav'rite of the Skies,
O born to Gifts by which the Noblest rise,
Improv'd in Arts by which the Brightest please,
Intent to Business, and polite for Ease;
Sublime in Eloquence, where loud Applause
Hath stil'd thee Patron of a Nation's Cause.
'Twas there the World perceiv'd and own'd thee great,
Thence ANNA call'd thee to the Reins of State;
Go, said the Greatest Queen, with OXFORD go,
And still the Tumults of the World below,
Exert thy Powers, and prosper; he that knows
To move with OXFORD never shou'd repose.
She spoke: the Patriot overspread thy Mind,
And all thy Days to publick Good resign'd.
Else might thy Soul so wonderfully wrought
For ev'ry depth and turn of curious Thought,
To this the Poet's sweet Recess retreat,
And thence report the Pleasures of the Seat,
Describe the Raptures which a Writer knows,
When in his Breast a Vein of Fancy glows,
Describe his Business while he works the Mine,
Describe his Temper when he sees it shine,
Or say when Readers easy Verse insnares,
How much the Writers Mind can act on theirs:
Whence Images in charming Numbers set,
A sort of Likeness in the Soul beget,
And what fair Visions oft we fancy nigh
By fond Delusions of the swimming Eye,
Or further pierce through Natures Maze to find
How Passions drawn give Passions to the Mind.

Oh what a sweet Confusion! what Surprize!
How quick the shifting Views of Pleasure rise!
While lightly skimming, with a transient Wing,
I touch the Beauties which I wish to sing.
Is Verse a sov'raign Regent of the Soul,
And fitted all its Motions to controul?
Or are they Sisters, tun'd at once above,
And shake like Unisons if either move?
For when the Numbers sing an eager Fight,
I've heard a Soldier's Voice express Delight;
I've seen his Eyes with crowding Spirits shine,

And round his Hilt his Hand unthinking twine.
When from the Shore the fickle Trojan flies,
And in sweet Measures poor Eliza dies,
I've seen the Book forsake the Virgins Hand,
And in their Eyes the Tears but hardly stand.
I've known them blush at soft Corinna's Name,
And in red Characters confess a Flame:
Or wish Success had more adorn'd his Arms,
Who gave the World for Cleopatra's Charms.

Ye Sons of Glory, be my first Appeal,
If here the Pow'r of Lines these Lines reveal.
When some great Youth has with impetuous Thought
Read o'er Atchievements which another wrought,
And seen his Courage and his Honour go
Through crowding Nations in Triumphant Show,
His Soul enchanted by the Words he reads
Shines all impregnated with sparkling Seeds,
And Courage here, and Honour there, appears
In brave Design that soars beyond his Years,
And this a Spear, and that a Chariot lends,
And War and Triumph he by turns attends:
Thus gallant Pleasures are his waking Dream,
Till some fair Cause have call'd him forth to Fame.
Then form'd to Life on what the Poet made,
And breathing Slaughter, and in Arms array'd,
He marches forward on the daring Foe,
And Emulation acts in ev'ry Blow.
Great Hector's Shade in Fancy stalks along,
From Rank to Rank amongst the Martial Throng,
While from his Acts he learns a Noble Rage,
And shines like Hector in the present Age.
Thus Verse will raise him to the Victor's Bays,
And Verse, that rais'd him, shall resound his Praise.

Ye tender Beauties, be my Witness too,
If Song can charm, and if my Song be true.
With sweet Experience oft a Fair may find
Her Passions mov'd by Passions well design'd;
And then she longs to meet a gentle Swain,
And longs to Love, and to be lov'd again.
And if by chance an Am'rous Youth appears,
With Pants and Blushes she the Courtship hears;
And finds a Tale that must with theirs agree,
And he's Septimius, and his Acme she:
Thus lost in Thought her melted Heart she gives,
And the rais'd Lover by the Poet lives.